Catherine van Valkenburg Waite

Adventures in the Far West

And life among the Mormons

Catherine van Valkenburg Waite

Adventures in the Far West
And life among the Mormons

ISBN/EAN: 9783337295233

Printed in Europe, USA, Canada, Australia, Japan

Cover: Foto ©Andreas Hilbeck / pixelio.de

More available books at **www.hansebooks.com**

ADVENTURES

IN THE

FAR WEST;

AND

LIFE AMONG THE MORMONS.

BY

MRS. C. V. WAITE.

Author of "THE MORMON PROPHET AND HIS HAREM," "THE LAW OF SOCIAL RETRIBUTION," "WOMAN'S POSITION IN CHURCH AND STATE," etc. etc.

CHICAGO:
C. V. WAITE AND COMPANY,
AND BOOK SELLERS GENERALLY.
1882.

Entered according to Act of Congress, in the year 1881, by
CATHARINE V. WAITE,
At the Library of Congress, in Washington.
All Rights reserved.

CONTENTS.

CHAPTER I.
PREPARING TO GO WEST.

                                                    PAGE

The Letter.—The Appointment.—Lake Park Seminary.—Packing up.—West of the Mississippi.—Uncle Sam's Boys.—Our Party........................ 1

CHAPTER II.
EXPERIENCES IN CAMP.

In Camp.—The Brinks.—Our Wagon.—Miss Julia.—The Professor.—"Home, Sweet Home."—Rest... 12

CHAPTER III.
NEW DIFFICULTIES.

We break down.—Jay Hawkers.—A Horrid Night.—Oyster Supper.—More Trouble.—Sunday on the Plains.—A Storm............................. 15

CONTENTS.

PAGE

CHAPTER IV.
PHILOSOPHY AND WATER.
The Little Blue.—Philosophical Discussion.—Crossing the Platte.—Nearly Drowned.—Over the River. 25

CHAPTER V.
WE JOURNEY ON.
An Indian Massacre.—Ash Hollow.—Wild Roses and Blood.—Climbing Scott's Bluff.- A Storm in Camp.—Ft. Laramie.—Our guest.—His Thrilling Story. 31

CHAPTER VI.
INCIDENTS OF TRAVEL.
Along the Platte.—Devil's Gate.—Rocky Mountains.-An Indian Princess.—Our Camp attacked by Indians.—In a State of Siege.—Burying our Dead.—Night Signals.—Terror.—We procure an Escort.—General Rejoicing.—Celebrating the 4th of July.—Oration of Judge Drave.—Dance on the Island. 42

CHAPTER VII.
CLOSING SCENES AND TRIALS.
Crossing Green River.—Hurrah for the Rope.—Ft. Bridger.—Needle Rock.—Wahsatch Mountains.—Emigration Canyon.—We behold the City of the Saints.—The Jordan River.—We arrive at Salt Lake City, and put up at the Townsend House. 59

CHAPTER VIII.
LIFE AMONG THE MORMONS.
Mormondom on the *Qui Vive*.—We go to Church.—We sit with the Prophet's Wives.—Miss Julia is de-

CONTENTS.

lighted.–We attend a Tea Party.—Distant Thunder.
—We visit Brother Brigham.—He shows the Cloven Foot... 68

CHAPTER IX.
WE GET BETTER ACQUAINTED WITH THE SAINTS.

Mormon Independence Day.—Anniversary Ball.—The New Governor and Brigham's Wives.—Miss Julia and the Prophet.—The Green-eyed Monster.—Trouble Brewing.—We are denounced in Church, and sent to H—ll Cross-lots.—Mrs. Burlingame and the Mormon Women.—Horrible Revelations.—Hand Cart Company—Apostasy.—He Fell Dead..... 83

CHAPTER X.
JOURNEY TO CARSON CITY.

Miss Julia Leaves Salt Lake.—Governor Doty and the Indians.—An Indian War Dance.—The Enchanted Cave.—A Mountain Lion.—Arrival at Carson..... 91

CHAPTER XI.
SAUNTERINGS AROUND THE HOLY CITY.

A Lovely Valley.—The Temple.—The Homes of the Principal Polygamists.—The Grand Harem.—The Prophet's Block.—The Court House.—The Council House.—The Arsenal.—The Nauvoo Legion.—Tithing.—Blood Atonement.—The Altar of Sacrifice.—Killing the Body to save the Soul............. 97

CHAPTER XII.
HAPPENINGS IN SALT LAKE CITY.

A Polygamous Community.—Mormon Wives are miserable.—A Flood of Tears.—The Temple.—Through the Endowments.—Setting the Women Free.—Gentilish.—We Visit a Patriarch with Five Wives and Twenty-one Children.—The Coming of the United States Troops.—Great Excitement.—Mobbing the Governor and Judges.—The Leaders forbid their "Women" to visit us........................ 106

CHAPTER XIII.

LIFE AT CAMP DOUGLAS.

Wives of the Officers.—Mrs. Reid, the Surgeon-General's Wife.—Excursion to Great Salt Lake.—A Dead Sea.—The Military Ball.—General Connor.—The Valley of the Salt Lake, from the Camp Observatory.—My Bitter Enemy................... 113

CHAPTER XIV

AN INSIDE VIEW OF THE PECULIAR INSTITUTION.

Mrs. Burlingame disguised as a mormon "sister."—House Hunting.—A Fiend in Human Form.—Chained in a Dark Cellar.—A Raving Maniac.—"I am starving."—Has your Husband taken a Second Wife? The "Proxy" Doctrine.—Married for Time.—Hard to marry two.—Married his Half-sister.—Married his Mother-in-law.—Inexorable Fate............... 120

CHAPTER XV.

A PROSPECTING EXPEDITION.

A Mysterious Visitor.—Six o'clock sharp.—He tells where to find the Gold.—We go in search.—Bingham Canyon rich as Cream.—We locate Claims.—First Mines ever

CONTENTS.

discovered by Gentiles in Utah............ 182

CHAPTER XVI.
MORMON MYSTERIES.

Marrying for Eternity.—The Endowment.—Baptism for the Dead.—Marrying for the Dead.—Raising up Children for their Dead.—Mormon Drama.—Dramatis Personæ.—Creation of the Earth.—"Let us make Man."—Garden of Eden.—Adam and Eve.—The Temptation.—The Fall.—Cursing the Serpent.—Restoration through Joseph Smith.—Grips, Key-words, Signs, and Oaths.—Cursing the United States Government..... 137

CHAPTER XVII.
HISTORY OF WOMAN.

The Ancient Rabbi and the Rib.—Heathen Opinions.—Adam a Polygamist.—Adam the Father of Jesus Christ.—Blasphemy.—The Bible and Polygamy.—Abraham and Sarah.—Jacob's Reward.—God rewards the Faithful with many Wives..................... 167

CHAPTER XVIII.
A SISTER'S REVELATION.

Deceiving Elders.—Teaching the Women the Revelation.—Refractory Wives.—Many First Wives Insane.—One tried to escape.—Attacked and murdered.—Gods and Goddesses.—Secret Orders............ 175

CHAPTER XIX.
A VISIT TO THE HAREM.

Plan of the Harem or Lion House.—Emeline the Light of the Harem.—Domestic Arrangements.—Aunt Fanny.—A Mormon Family.—What the Women do.—Brigham

at Home.—The Theater.—The Garden and Orchard.—
A Lovely Home.—"The Trail of the Serpent."   185

CHAPTER XX.
THE WIVES OF THE PROPHET.

Brigham Young and his Family.—A Courtship.—Hiram
conquers.—A Model Son.—Lucy Decker Seely, First
Wife in "Plurality."—Governor Harding flirting with
the Wives.—Plurals.—Vilate Cole.—Father and Daugh-
ter.—Eliza R. Snow, the Sweet Singer of Israel.—Clara
Chase, the Maniac.—Mrs. Cobb, a Boston Lady.—Ame-
lia.—How the Prophet won her.—Amelia's Lovers.—
A dangerous Rival.—Miss Selima Ursenbach.—The
Prophet in love the thirtieth Time.—Fooled by the little
God Cupid..........................   200

CHAPTER XXI.
THE SECRET ORDERS.

Our Visitor.—His Story.—Apostates.—The Gladdenites.—
—Persecuting Apostates.—The Morrisites.—Brigham's
Sermon.—The Bombardment.—The Massacre.—The
Mormon Theocracy.—The Priesthoods.—The Archees.
—The Danites.—Gods and Goddesses.—Dr. Sprague.—
John D. Lee.—The Sword of the Almighty.—Mormon
Murders.—Noted Danites.................   233

CHAPTER XXII.
SOCIETY IN THE SIERRAS.

Miss Julia's Letter.—We are all Squires.—New Year's Cal-
lers.—"A Dead Thing."—The Rival Candidates.—The
Skylight District.—Col. Sellers.—The Comstock.—A
Delightful Ride.—Julia goes to San Francisco.—Her
Admirers.—A San Francisco Lawyer gets the Prize.—
The Wedding........................   262

CHAPTER XXIII.
ARRIVAL OF THE JOSEPHITE MISSIONARIES.

Founding a Colony for the Morrisites.—Mr. Burlingame leaves Salt Lake City.—Elder Briggs.—True Latter Day Saints.—Their Creed.—Brigham a Pretender.—"The Fullness of Time."—Down with Polygamy and Blood Atonement.—Persecuting the Josephites.—They preach in Mrs. Burlingame's House.—Attempt to burn down the House.—Brigham and Gen. Connor.—The Flag of Distress.—Mrs. Burlingame and the Josephites leave the City with Military Escorts.—Farewell to the poor and suffering Sisters.—Despair or Indifference.—In Search of new Adventures.

APPENDIX.
A PANORAMIC VIEW OF MORMONISM.

Chronological History.—Mormon War.—Anti Polygamy Bill.—Garfield and the Mormons.—Guiteau a Mormon.—Was Garfield shot by order of the Mormon Authorities?—Circumstantial Evidence.—Will the Edmunds Bill be enforced?—Brigham Young STILL ALIVE.

CONTENTS.

at Home.—The Theater.—The Garden and Orchard.—
A Lovely Home.—"The Trail of the Serpent." 185

CHAPTER XX.
THE WIVES OF THE PROPHET.

Brigham Young and his Family.—A Courtship.—Hiram
conquers.—A Model Son.—Lucy Decker Seely, First
Wife in "Plurality."—Governor Harding flirting with
the Wives.—Plurals.—Vilate Cole.—Father and Daughter.—Eliza R. Snow, the Sweet Singer of Israel.—Clara
Chase, the Maniac.—Mrs. Cobb, a Boston Lady.—Amelia.—How the Prophet won her.—Amelia's Lovers.—
A dangerous Rival.—Miss Selima Ursenbach.—The
Prophet in love the thirtieth Time.—Fooled by the little
God Cupid........................ 200

CHAPTER XXI.
THE SECRET ORDERS.

Our Visitor.—His Story.—Apostates.—The Gladdenites.—
—Persecuting Apostates.—The Morrisites.—Brigham's
Sermon.—The Bombardment.—The Massacre.—The
Mormon Theocracy.—The Priesthoods.—The Archees.
—The Danites.—Gods and Goddesses.—Dr. Sprague.—
John D. Lee.—The Sword of the Almighty.—Mormon
Murders.—Noted Danites................ 233

CHAPTER XXII.
SOCIETY IN THE SIERRAS.

Miss Julia's Letter.—We are all Squires.—New Year's Callers.—"A Dead Thing."—The Rival Candidates.—The
Skylight District.—Col. Sellers.—The Comstock.—A
Delightful Ride.—Julia goes to San Francisco.—Her
Admirers.—A San Francisco Lawyer gets the Prize.—
The Wedding....................... 262

CONTENTS.

PAGE

CHAPTER XXIII.
ARRIVAL OF THE JOSEPHITE MISSIONARIES.

Founding a Colony for the Morrisites.—Mr. Burlingame leaves Salt Lake City.—Elder Briggs.—True Latter Day Saints.—Their Creed.—Brigham a Pretender.—"The Fullness of Time."—Down with Polygamy and Blood Atonement.—Persecuting the Josephites.—They preach in Mrs. Burlingame's House.—Attempt to burn down the House.—Brigham and Gen. Connor.—The Flag of Distress.—Mrs. Burlingame and the Josephites leave the City with Military Escorts.—Farewell to the poor and suffering Sisters.—Despair or Indifference.—In Search of new Adventures.

APPENDIX.
A PANORAMIC VIEW OF MORMONISM.

Chronological History.—Mormon War.—Anti Polygamy Bill.—Garfield and the Mormons.—Guiteau a Mormon. —Was Garfield shot by order of the Mormon Authorities?—Circumstantial Evidence.—Will the Edmunds Bill be enforced?—Brigham Young STILL ALIVE.

ADVENTURES IN THE FAR WEST.

CHAPTER -I.

"Will you go?"

"Where?"

"To the Far West."

"Yes, if we can have a pleasant company and a jolly time."

The first speaker held in her hand an open letter, and her question was based upon its contents. The second speaker was a young lady, enthusiastic, brilliant and fond of adventure.

The first gun had been fired upon Fort Sumpter, and the dark cloud of war over-shadowed the land. Trade, commerce and all kinds of business were deranged, and many saw before them nothing but enlistment or financial distress. The country was just beginning to recover from the panic of 1857, but the cry "to arms," sounded the death knell of the new prosperity. Men's minds were unsettled and all eagerly grasped at something new.

Mr. Burlingame was a prominent lawyer in the Garden City of the West. He was sitting one day in his office, thinking how he would avert the calamity which threatened to sweep all before it, when a friend entered.

"I am glad to see you Mr. Secretary, and have just been thinking of you, and of the desperate condition of our unhappy country. The law business will be entirely prostrated during the war."

"Come with me," said the Secretary, "and we will find something for you to do, to keep you out of mischief."

In three hours from this conversation, the parties were *en route* to Washington. Mr. Burlingame called upon President Lincoln, with whom he had long been on terms of intimacy, and told him his errand.

After a pleasant chat and many reminiscences of "riding the circuit" in Illinois, in the early day, Mr. Lincoln said, "I can't give you the place you want, for old Judge S. and I used to sleep together, but I'll see what I can do for you."

In a week or so, the Secretary met Mr. Burlingame and told him "Old Abe" wanted to see him. Mr. Burlingame lost no time in calling at the White House.

He found Mr. Lincoln in the best of humor and, after a few pleasantries, he said:

"You have been an old-line Abolitionist, and have a "heap of grit," for your size. Now I want somebody to go out to Utah, to keep the "saints" in order. I have got to send a "new lot," and you can go, if you feel like it. The saints are rather fractious. They have just horsewhipped Governor D. and sent him home, and have made it too hot for the rest, but I mean to send some men, this time, that they can't scare."

"Well, Mr. President," said Mr. Burlingame "this is a horse of another color, and looks a little warlike. I'll think about it and let you know."

"All right," said the kind-hearted President and they parted.

Mr. Burlingame immediately wrote to his wife, to know if she would accompany him, in case he accepted the place.

Mrs. Burlingame and Miss Julia, the sister of Mr. Burlingame, were the speakers. They now discussed the plan, and the novelty of the journey, the radical change that it would bring from the daily round of school work, housekeeping, etc., proved too much for them to resist, and they decided to go. Accordingly, a letter was despatched to Washington; Mr. Burlingame accepted the position, and immediately turned his face homeward.

The arrival of Mr. Burlingame at Lake Park Seminary created no little excitement among its occupants. The Seminary was advertised for rent, "furnished," and the school to be carried on by the lessee.

Groups of young ladies were to be seen almost everywhere, discussing the situation. Some said they didn't believe Mrs. Burlingame and Miss Julia would go at all. This would all blow over in a few days and everything would go on as usual.

"If you think," said Clara Wilbur, "that our Principal is that kind of a woman, you are mistaken in her. She will go, and you may as well make up your minds to have another teacher."

"I don't see what Miss Julia wants to go away out there among those dreadful Mormons for, any way," said sweet Nellie Mayo. "I think she has a real nice time, now."

"That's all you know about it," snapped Clara, "I don't blame her one bit for going; she's tired of hearing bad lessons and living such a humdrum kind of life. I'd go, too, if I had the chance."

Several answers came to the advertisement

and the choice fell upon a minister of the Episcopal Church. The young ladies were quite reconciled when they found they were to have a gentleman for Principal, and voted him a 'love of a man.'

Clara Wilbur. with her usual sagacity, said, "You'll find you won't like him. You'll find we've caught a "Tartar."

The Trustees and minister remonstrated with Mrs. Burlingame against going: but it was no use, her mind was made up, and she said, she never put her hand to the plow and turned back.

The Seminary disposed of, the Burlingames turned their attention to getting ready "to cross the plains."

A council of war was held, and it was decided not to go without everything, but to try and make the journey comfortable. Mrs. Burlingame thought that the common emigrant wagon was too small for family use. Mr. B. immediately proposed to have one built to her order, that should combine comfort with safety, and insure a delightful trip. They were to go by cars to the Missouri river, and thence by wagons to Salt Lake City, a distance of over one thousand miles.

The question of next importance was what to take, but it soon resolved itself into the more difficult one of what to leave. A family of seven were to be provided with bedding, clothing, provisions, medicines and all the etceteras, which belong to family life. One wagon was to convey all these things besides the seven persons.

"Miss Julia," said Mrs. Burlingame, "I wish you would come and give your opinion. The cook thinks we must have this barrel full of cooking utensils and they are too heavy. "Well mum," said Bridget, "sure an ye must ate, an ye must drink an sure ye must have things to bake, fry and boil with." "The fiat has gone forth," said Miss Julia, "and the things must go." The laundress next gave it as her opinion that very few cooking things would do but people must keep clean, and that two wash tubs, a wash board and two flats were little enough in all conscience. Thus, through all departments of housekeeping and after many weary and perplexing days, the packing was done. Other arrangements went on well. The vehicle was built and forwarded to the Missouri River, as was most of the freight.

Now, it was plain that good, stout steeds would be needed to propel the aforesaid vehicle, and as Mr. Vane was a good judge of horse flesh, he agreed to precede the party and to meet them at the Missouri with the required animals.

The whole party were to go as suited them best, and meet upon a certain fixed day at the Missouri River.

Miss Julia had gone to visit friends on the way and would join them at Hannibal. Missouri.

I find the following in Mrs. Burlingame's diary.

May 5, 1862.

"On this beautiful spring morning, I find myself all ready, with my little family, to enter upon a long and perilous journey, through a country inhabited by Indians and swarming with wild beasts.

I believe I am in the path of duty and shall go forth with a light heart and a firm tread."

"It is all over. The parting adieus have been said and we are riding along in the luxurious cars of the Chicago, Burlington & Quincy R.R. as if we were on a pleasure trip."

Tuesday, May 6th.

We arrived all right, this evening, at the Barrett House, Burlington, Iowa, have had a good supper and are feeling much refreshed. A government officer has just called at the hotel to inspect our baggage. This red-tape operation and the remark that a government "fleet" was expected down during the night, were the only circumstances to remind us of war; except that we met a regiment of soldiers at East Burlington.

We have had calls from some very pleasant friends, this evening, and shall feel quite refreshed to renew our journey, on the morrow.

Thursday, May 8th.

Yesterday morning, we took the packet, "Jenny Whipple," and had a pleasant ride down the Mississippi to Fort Madison, my former home.

It seems good to meet with the tried and true friends who were so kind and generous to me, when I came among them, years ago, as a country school ma'am.

At my brother's hospitable mansion, we are receiving and entertaining our friends, and having a season of social enjoyment that will long be remembered.

Friday, May 9th.

Parting with our kind friends and dear relatives at Fort Madison, we took boat for Hannibal, Missouri. Here we found sister Julia awaiting us. Our freight being all right, we made haste to catch the train for St. Joseph and, as I write, we are smoothly gliding along over the Hannibal & St. Joe R.R., enjoying the balmy breath of spring, in this mild climate, and inhaling the odors of the blossoming woods, fragrant with a wealth of wild fruits and flowers.

At several points on the route, Companies of

soldiers are encamped to guard the R.R. track, which forcibly reminds us that we are in the "enemy's country."

The children are having a gay time and enjoying the ride immensely. Some gentlemen have just brought in, for them, large branches of dogwood and red bud blossoms. They are in ecstasies over the red and white flowers and are wildly exclaiming, "Mamma!" "Auntie!" "How beautiful they look, and how sweet they smell!"

While the children have been enjoying themselves with the flowers, sister Julia and I have been getting dinner on the cars. We have a little spirit lamp, so arranged that we can made tea on it, and, but for the danger of its oversetting and exploding with the motion of the cars, we can do very well with it. We have our lunch basket, well stored; and, with a good cup of tea, we have made out a very comfortable meal.

What a great convenience it would be to have a dining car attached to the train. It is almost impossible to get out to meals, with children, at the eating stations.

We are now drawing near the mighty Missouri, which, I think, ought to be called "the Father of Waters," rather than the Mississippi. Rising in the very heart of the Rocky Mountains, and rolling in majestic grandeur to its union with the Mississippi, whose destiny and character it changes and controls, it is truly the great arterial current of this continent. Strong, turbulent and unmanageable, it is a fitting exponent of one of the most powerful elements in nature.

Saturday, May 10th.

We arrived Friday evening at St. Joseph, Missouri, and are stopping at the Patee House.

It is a great luxury to find a pleasant, home-like hotel, and to have every want attended to by careful, well-trained servants. We are resting and preparing for the fatigues of the journey before us.

Our party are arriving one after another. This evening, my brother, Mr. Vane, came in with the horses. They are nice ones and will, I hope, prove equal to the task before them. Mr. Brink, who is to conduct our train across the plains, is here with his family. Judge Drave, Mr. Burlingame's associate, has also arrived. He is an old gentleman, but very pleasant and of a courtly demeanor, reminding one of "ye judges of ye olden time." The flowing and powdered wig and the judicial robes, would well become this stately and dignified man of "Roman mien."

Ex-Alderman Saxton and Mr. Perry, who are

en route to the Sandwich Islands for their health, are here. Mr. Braddish, a Chicago lawyer, with his wife and son, are to be of our party and are hourly expected. Sister Julia tells me that Professor Goodhue and Mr. Belfield, whom she met in St. Louis, are to join our party. Prof. Goodhue is interested in the geology of the country; and Mr. Belfield is connected with the Press. We are anticipating a very pleasant journey, having, as we think, unusually pleasant company.

We are looking for Gov. H., who has agreed to join us here.

We are having a very pleasant time in St. Joe. Mr. Vane and Mr. Burlingame are preparing everything necessary for camp life. We are going into camp in two or three days. We are receiving every attention and assistance from the citizens. This is an enterprising and growing city, and bids fair to be one of the largest cities of the West.

The children, especially little Madge, the baby, have been ailing, and I dread the journey on their account. I have been told, however, that camp life is very good for children and that they will stand this mode of travel better than an adult.

Well! we shall soon have to try the realities of "Camp Life."

CHAPTER II.

IN CAMP.

The sun rose on this May morning like a ball of fire. Early, he sent up rays of red and purple, which faded, before his majestic arrival, into a dull glare.

About nine o' clock, it was announced that the carriage was ready to take the ladies into camp. With an undefinable dread, they gathered up their things, got the children ready, and left the hotel, which had been their pleasant home for several days, and proceeded to the camp.

In the camp, all was bustle and confusion. The Brinks were at breakfast. A long, low table, made of two wide planks, so arranged as to fold up and slip easily into the wagon, was furnished with tin cups and platters, steel forks and pewter spoons. The food was equally plain, consisting of coffee, black, that is, without cream, bacon, beans and hard bread. Not a superfluous article was to be seen in any direction.

The Brinks had crossed the plains a number of times. The meal over, everything was put away in a few minutes, ready for a start. The vehicle, in which Mr. Burlingame was to convey his family, was the centre of attraction. The common emigrant wagon would almost go inside of it. Beside being much longer and higher than the common wagon, it was set up on springs, which made it tower above all surrounding objects. It was so arranged inside, that by placing slats across, very comfortable beds could be made up. Boxes for provisions were arranged along the sides and served also for seats during the day.

The Burlingames had all kinds of provisions and everything to make them comfortable, and yet they were not without a secret misgiving, that, after all, they were not so well prepared for their journey as their more experienced companions.

Four horses were required to draw this outfit and Mr. Burlingame, Mr. Vane and Hardin, the driver, were busy getting their teams ready for a start. It is no easy matter to get four horses, total strangers to each other, to work together. One chafed under the harness and would not be comforted; another was fractious and would not draw. After great difficulty and much exhaustion, under a boiling sun, the Burlingame outfit got under way.

The party crossed the Missouri River to Elwood, and after traveling about seven miles, over roads full of ruts and holes, encamped for the night.

The extreme heat was followed by a sharp frost and chilly atmosphere, which was very trying to our travelers on this first night in camp. However, they made the best of it, and, as they were encamped in a lovely spot, they made up a rousing fire, and, gathering round it after supper, the more experienced of the party tried to cheer up the novices and bade them hope for the best.

As they were all seated round the fire, telling stories of adventures this one and that had met with in days gone by, the Professor, who was conversing with Miss Julia, no doubt upon the geological formation of the country, suddenly espied something, which, upon examination proved to be a guitar.

All eyes were at once directed to Miss Julia, and "A song, a song," echoed and re-echoed from all sides. Miss Julia took the instrument, and in her own inimitable style, sang, "Home, Sweet Home." As the tender and touching strains floated upon the clear air, in that wild and lonely spot, every eye moistened and every heart grew sad. As the fire grew low, and the stars brighter, "Good Night," was said, and the travelers retired to rest.

CHAPTER III.

NEW DIFFICULTIES.

A good night's rest and a warm breakfast gave our travelers fresh courage and the whole camp was in motion at a very early hour. The Burlingames, having a more elaborate outfit, were rather behind the balance of the train in getting started. They made very good time until they reached Troy. Here they stopped to take on horse-feed. Mules will live where horses will starve; the latter must have grain to enable them to work, while mules will do very well on grass.

In addition to the heavy load already on, Mr. Burlingame took on about 500 pounds of horse-feed. This was put mainly on the front axle. The roads were very full of ruts and they had not gone more than two miles, when the wagon struck a deep rut, a crash was heard, and the bolster over the forward axle-tree broke in the centre. Thus disabled, there was nothing to do but to send back to Troy and have a new axle-tree made, but, as this was not to be done in a minute, the Burlingames could go no farther. Their party had gone on ahead, and they remained alone, all day and night, on the lonely road, in the midst of the Jay-Hawkers of Kansas.

This accident greatly disheartened Mrs. Burlingame and Miss Julia, but they resolved to be brave and go ahead, never dreaming that this was but as a drop to the ocean, in comparison to what they were yet to endure.

Knowing nothing of the dangers and difficulties of the way, they had but little to fear. but had they known what was in store for them, they would have gone back at once, and this history would never have been written. Towards night, the new bolster was completed and placed in position, but too late to go on. But little sleep was had by any one on this, their second night in camp. The first was wild, weird and solemn, but the second was terrible in its utter loneliness, and in the fear of danger from surrounding enemies. "What if the Jay-Hawkers should steal our horses," said Miss Julia. "In Heaven's name, what should we do?" "Hark! Hush!" whispered Mrs. Burlingame, "I hear somebody coming. I do believe we shall have our horses stolen and, perhaps, lose our own lives."

Mr. Burlingame and Hardin kept vigilant watch, by turns, but three o'clock came and no Jay Hawker. So the ladies prepared an early breakfast and, all things being ready, they started on, about five o'clock, and drove about eighteen miles, where they found the remainder of the party awaiting them.

By this time, it had become evident that the Burlingame outfit was entirely too comfortable, and something must be done or they would never reach their destination. A council was held in camp, in which it was decided to metamorphose the aforesaid vehicle. Accordingly, the upper part of the wagon-bed was taken out and the wagon-bed and top made shorter and narrower. The ladies were told that the wagon must be lightened, and that they must throw the heaviest things overboard.

"Just to think," said Miss Julia, "after all the time we spent selecting and packing, that we now have got to throw away everything. It is too bad. Why didn't we have two small wagons and then we could have had one for the things, and one for the family."

"Dear me," said Mrs. Burlingame, "it is a sad condition we are in, but we must make the best of it and get through somehow."

With this, she commenced lightening up and the cooking utensils, wash-tubs, flatirons, etc., were cast out with right good will. About half the feed was also left behind, for some more experienced emigrant to pick up. Thus trimmed and reefed, the ship sailed on over the prairies, but fresh troubles awaited our unfortunate party.

After all was done, and the bill of repairs paid, Mr. Burlingame said to his wife, "My dear, the gentlemen of the party have been very kind and have assisted me very much in rigging up the old ship, suppose we give an oyster supper."

"A capital idea," assented Mrs. Burlingame, "and quite a novelty, an oyster supper on the plains. It shall be done."

Great preparations were made. The supper was laid in style, the white napery and silver brought out and, with all the drawbacks, the table did look splendidly.

The ladies of the party all assisted. The gentlemen put on society manners and were as polite and attentive to the ladies, as if they were in an elegant drawing-room. Everybody forgot the troubles of the past and voted the party an unrivalled success.

Having remodeled the wagon, and lightened

the load by throwing away many pounds of superfluous matter, such as flatirons, washtubs, kettles and about two hundred pounds of horse-feed, our travelers flattered themselves that everything would now go on smoothly and that their troubles were at an end.

The following, from the Journal of Mr. Burlingame, will show how soon their hopes were to be blasted, and in how many unexpected ways troubles came upon them.

Wednesday, May 21.

This morning, the horse, George, was taken sick, apparently with the cholic. We drenched him and started on, leaving camp at half past nine A. M.

Traveled about eighteen miles and encamped near a stream of water. Here, a serious accident happened, entirely disabling our best horse. He took fright at a tin bucket, which the driver was carrying on his back with water for the camp, and ran, tearing the saddle to pieces, cutting his fore foot badly and spraining his hips and perhaps his spine. He is so badly injured that I fear it will be impossible for us to travel with him, for several days. To complete the chapter of accidents, I left my revolver at Kinnikuk, and was obliged to go back, three miles, after it, at ten o'clock at night,

We stopped so long at Kinnikuk, to get our wagon fixed that we were late in making camp. The weather was cold, and damp; altogether, we had a hard night of it.

Thursday, May 22.

To-day, we managed to go fifteen miles with our injured horse. We stopped at the house of a Mr. McRay, where we stayed all night, and next morning, traded off Rufus, the lame horse, for a black mare, worth about eighty dollars, giving forty dollars to boot. Before the accident, Rufus was well worth one hundred and fifty dollars. We were all attached to him and parted from the poor fellow with many regrets.

We found Mr. McRay a good specimen of prairie borderer, frank, good-natured and warm-hearted, but looking out pretty sharply for the main chance. For supper, breakfast, and lodging, we gave him a feather bed and a blanket.

Friday, May 23.

To-day, we drove, with our newly organized team, eighteen miles, to Seneca, the county seat of Nemaha county, where we encamped for the night. George still remaining sick, we decided to buy another horse, if possible, and put George under the saddle.

Saturday, May 24.

Bought a new horse, this morning, for ninety

dollars, and pushed on to Vermillion Creek, twenty-four miles. Here we overtook the party of W. H. Russell, of Lexington, Mo. They are a pleasant and intelligent party, provided with all the conveniences for camp life. We encamped in a beautiful grove, on Vermillion Creek, having now traveled about one hundred miles from St. Joe, in seven days.

Sunday, May 25.

This is a beautiful Sunday morning. With the bright sun sending his warm rays down through the trees, and the breeze playing freshly among them, we cheerfully prepare our breakfast and get ready to proceed on our journey. It is not our intention to travel on Sunday, but we have got behind our train and are obliged to take this day to overtake them.

Later. We have traveled twelve miles since, over a road, rough, but otherwise good, and are encamped with Brink's company, near Morrisville. During the eight days that we have traveled, we have only made camp with our party twice. We have been exposed to the Kansas Jay Hawkers and other stray outlaws that infest this country, but have been unmolested, so far.

The ladies have been wonderfully sick of their romantic journey and would gladly return to

Chicago, if they could. Mrs. B. says she certainly would go back, if she had not told the "minister," when he prophesied her return, that she "never put her hand to the plow and turned back." Considering the trials and difficulties we have encountered, the ladies have certainly shown remarkable endurance and determination.

Monday, May 26.

This morning, I was obliged to get one of the horses shod, which delayed us so long that we again got behind our train. Brink pushed on to Rocky Creek, thirty miles. We traveled about twenty-three miles and encamped with a small party of emigrants, with whom we had traveled occasionally, for several days.

These people were from Missouri and Arkansas, and were leaving their homes on account of the war, to seek new ones in California and Oregon. They belonged to the class known as poor whites, and were about as destitute of worldly goods as they could well be. They had cows yoked together for teams, in some cases, and several families clubbed together and carried their outfit in one "Prairie Schooner."

The men, women and children, most of them walked, and when they struck camp, they milked the cows and baked "corn dodgers," for their supper. We found many kind hearts beneath

STORM ON THE PLAINS.

their rough exteriors, and they were ever ready to extend a helping hand. We bought milk of them, and, as 'misery loves company,' we struck up quite a friendship for each other.

Tuesday, May 28.

We encamped last night on the open prairie, on a sloping hill side. The weather was very sultry, and the muttering thunder and vivid lightning portended the coming storm. We had often heard of the terrible storms of wind and rain on the plains, but our preconceived ideas paled before the dreadful reality. After all was arranged for the night and the horses made fast to the wagon for fear of a "stampede," we tried to sleep but the prospect of the coming storm prevented. About ten o'clock the storm broke forth upon us with all its fury. The wind blew a perfect hurricane, the rain fell in torrents and the inky darkness was only relieved by the vivid flashes of lightning.

The horses being fastened on the lower side of the wagon, made frantic efforts to get loose, which came near oversetting the wagon. I clung with all my might to the upper hind wheel on the outside, while the ladies threw all their weight on the inside at the same point.

The combined roar of the wind and rain was so great that I could not make the ladies hear my voice, just inside the wagon, though I shouted with all the power of my lungs, holding the wagon cover open at the same time. The tent had blown down, instantly, at the beginning of the storm, and Hardin the driver was under, and managed to hold it down over him, thus keeping himself dry and comfortable and leaving me to manage the best I could. When I asked him why he did not come out and help me, he said; "I was taking care of the tent."

I shuddered to think what the consequences would have been if the wagon had been blown over, and women and children thrown under the feet of four horses, and a roaring torrent rushing headlong a few rods distant.

As soon as we could see, we gathered up our scattered traps, and though drenched to the skin, harnessed up before breakfast and drove on Rock Creek seven miles, when we found our company in camp.

We found that our friends had encountered a storm, but nothing like as violent as the one we had witnessed, as they were on the timber.

We dried our clothing and bedding, cooked and ate a good warm breakfast and drove on the Little Sandy fifteen miles, near which we encamped for the night.

Here we had a good night's rest, and hoping

we were at last through with the worst of our accidents and fatigues, we started fresh upon our journey.

CHAPTER IV.

PHILOSOPHY AND WATER.

The Little Blue is a beautiful stream of pure water and flows gently along between banks covered with verdure, and fragrant with wild fruits and flowers. Our weary travelers enjoyed the picturesque scenery greatly, and in their enjoyment of the present, forgot the horrors of the past.

After a delightful day, they encamped in a lovely grove, on the banks of the river.

Only those who have passed through similar experiences, can fully understand how perfectly happy our company were, when, after a good supper, they gathered round the glowing camp fire.

Miss Julia, for the first time in many days, brought out her guitar and sang several of her sweetest songs. All were entranced; the music, the solemn stillness, the quiet stars looking down upon this little handful of people, far from the busy haunts of men, cast a shadow over all and for a few moments no one uttered a word.

The Professor was the first to break the spell. He said, "In moments like these, how man sinks into insignificance! How nature surrounds and absorbs him! A mere speck on her bosom, he is wholly dependent on his generous mother, Earth. He appears upon the scene, frets out his brief day, disappears; and the stars shine on, the earth revolves, nature smiles and frowns as usual, and scarce a ripple is produced on the broad ocean of time to note that he has either lived or died."

"I had supposed," said Miss Julia, "that man, instead of being a mere accident of nature, was her highest form and crowning act, and combined in himself, the Universe; that all nature was made for him and that this earth was thrown into its orbit, with its days and nights, its seasons and harvests, its golden treasures, its azure skies and sparkling waters, to minister to the wants and tastes of the beings who came from the hand of Deity, pure, noble and God-like.'

While Miss Julia was giving utterance to these sentiments, her lovely face was lighted up with a glow of enthusiasm, her cheeks were the color of the wild roses that perfumed the valley, and her eyes shone with intense luster.

After a little rustle of sympathy and satisfaction among the company, a slight pause ensued and all eyes were turned to Judge Drave.

With a dignified smile he turned to Miss Julia and said, "My dear Miss Burlingame, your sentiments reflect great credit upon both head and heart; but allow one who has seen nearly three score and ten years, to express an opinion somewhat different from your own." She bowed her head with reverence and the Judge continued, "When the Great Creator called into existence the worlds and systems of worlds which constitute the Universe, He did it not for the happiness or comfort of so insignificant a factor as man, but for his own glory and aggrandizement. Should man, as a part of this Universe, refuse to place himself in harmony with the Divine will, his place will be filled by other and nobler beings, and he destroyed forever."

As no one ventured to express an opinion contrary to this, the subject turned to lighter themes and after a delightful evening, the company retired to rest, beneath the spreading branches of the forest.

For several days, our travelers have journeyed on, meeting with no serious trouble and having the usual incidents of camp life. They have been traversing "The Divide," as it is called, between the Little Blue and the Platte.

On the 1st of June, they reached Fort Kearney, and were hospitably received and entertained by Captain Thompson and his estimable lady. To those who have all their lives been accustomed to the comforts and refinements of life, there is no sight more pleasing, after having been denied them, than a clean, well kept house and a bounteous and well spread table. Our travelers enjoyed the generous hospitality of the Fort, and continued their journey with hearts filled with gratitude to their kind friends.

On the 7th day of June, the party reached the Platte River. They found it swollen from the June freshets and rising rapidly. A consultation was held as to whether they should make a ford, and cross at this point, or go on to Julesburg, the regular ford.

As the river was rising at the rate of six inches in twenty-four hours, they considered it dangerous to delay and they proceeded to dig away the bank to make a road. Mr. Brink had a pair of large mules and he was to lead off, and Mr. Burlingame's four horse team was to follow.

All being ready, the ladies sitting upon the boxes inside the wagon, holding the children, the Burlingame outfit plunged in. The front wheels went down with a crash, the water poured into the wagon bed in torrents and the horses were almost submerged. Mr. Burlingame was riding one of the horses, and as the horse he was riding fell, Mr. B. jumped from his back on to the front leader, and by guiding him carefully, managed to start the whole team. They had proceeded only a few rods, when the wagon was so clogged by the quicksands which the swift current carried against the wheels, that the horses could no longer move it.

Here was a dilemma indeed, a wagon so deeply imbedded in quicksand that four horses could not move it, and the sand rapidly accumulating. The party on shore were anxiously watching with their glasses and, seeing the danger, a number of the gentlemen rode into the river to render assistance. They jumped from their horses in the midst of the roaring current, put their shoulders to the wheels of the wagon and, raising them out of the sand, enabled the horses to move on.

In this way they worked, until a new difficulty presented itself. They were losing the ford. The horses were beginning to swim. As this course was certain destruction, Mr. Burlingame jumped from the horse into the water, to hunt for the ford. He would swim first in one direction, then in another, till he could find bottom, and would then order an advance. The good friends would raise the wheels out of the quicksands, the noble steeds give a spring and on they would go for a few rods, until out of breath. The party on shore watched every movement with breathless anxiety, and expected every moment to see wagon, horses and men carried away by the almost resistless current.

Mrs. B., Miss Julia and the children remained inside, in silent terror. Mrs. B. gave one scream when her husband jumped into the river. Miss Julia displayed great presence of mind and kept the children quiet by a resort, first to punishment and then to the sugar bowl. ' Mrs. B. was so wholly absorbed by the terrors of the situation, that, as Miss Julia afterward said, "she did not notice me when I chastised the baby, Lucie, though I sat by her side." "By the aid of our heroic and daring friends, and our good, stout steeds," Mrs. B. wrote to a friend, "we were at length rescued from a watery grave, and after being in the river an hour and a half, we landed on the opposite side of the treacherous Platte."

CHAPTER V.

AN INDIAN MASSACRE.

The sun rose on the morning of June 8th, on our travelers in camp on the north side of the Platte. The day was bright and beautiful and, as it was the Sabbath, it was spent in resting from the fatigues of the day before. A member of the company decided to return to Chicago, and many letters were entrusted to his care. The Post-Offices in this region are few and far between.

As the train was moving along, next day, June 9th, everything working well and everybody in good spirits, the sky was suddenly overcast. The violet clouds portended a storm of hail and wind.

Nothing is more dreaded on these plains than these wind and hail storms. The train halted and commenced preparing for the storm. The corners of the wagons were put towards the wind, the tents pitched and guyed down, the guy ropes fastened to the wagons and ditches dug around the tents. With eager eyes the travelers watched the advancing cloud; but suddenly the wind changed, the cloud sailed away, and instead of the dreaded storm, a most beautiful rainbow spanned the entire heavens from N. E. to S. E., extending upwards, at least half way to the zenith. The colors were most brilliant and the whole background of a settled darkness, setting off the rainbow to the best advantage. Add to this a shadow or second rainbow, near the first, outside of the ring, and not quite so brilliant, and the whole was a picture never to be forgotten, and worth going many miles to see.

For several days the road lay among sand hills, no house, no signs of life; nothing but the hot sun looking down, and scorching every thing he touched. They had traveled thus through sand, sand, sand, for many weary miles, with the muddy Platte a little to the right, when suddenly they came upon some beautiful springs, opening from the side of the sand hills. The horses and mules, equally with the travelers, enjoyed the cooling draughts. In these days of railroads, the traveler can form no just estimate of the hardships and privations endured by those who made the journey overland twenty years ago.

While the general outline of this country is a sandy, desolate plain, occasionally there is a bit of scenery that rivals, in beauty, any thing found in the world. Ash Hollow is such a sweet little spot. A clear and purling stream flows gently along at the foot of the hills, the sides of which are covered with the most lovely wild roses. The butterflies flit from flower to flower, unconscious of the presence of human beings. Little springs gush out along the hill sides, leaving in their track most delicate green tapestry. A sense of coolness and freshness overcomes all sense of fatigue and heat, and the traveler feels that he could remain here always and be happy.

It was here that the rude children of nature had pitched their tents and were resting after a long hunting excursion, when they were overtaken and surprised by General Harney and his men, and an indiscriminate slaughter ensued. Men, women and children were slain, with scarcely enough left to carry the news to the next tribe. Such treatment as this has made for the people and government a great deal of trouble, for the Indians class all whites together and take revenge upon any white person they may meet. In the great majority of instances, the difficulties with the Indians have been traced to some overt act on the part of the whites.

Our travelers had now passed nearly a week in traveling these arid and sandy plains. They had carried water and food, and would have suffered much from thirst, but for the springs that occasionally were found flowing from the sand hills. They came again into the Stage Road, which they had left when they crossed the Platte, a little east of Court House Rock Station, and about 75 miles north-west of Julesburg. For one week, they had seen no house, or other sign of civilization, except a few emigrants, who, like themselves, were taking the cut-off.

From Mr. Burlingame's Journal.
Saturday June 14.

We made camp to-night near Scott's Bluffs. These Bluffs are 50 miles southeast of Ft. Laramie, and are the first indications of the rugged and mountainous country into which we are about to enter. They are about 500 feet high, very broken and picturesque in appearance, and present to the traveler a great variety of wild and beautiful scenery.

Sunday June 15.

This afternoon I started from camp to make the ascent of the bluffs. After an hour's walk I arrived at their feet, but the problem confronted me of how to reach the top. In front of me and for some distance on either side arose perpendicular walls of rock, entirely inaccessible.

However, by examining a little more closely, I found that a few straggling cedars ran up the mountain in two or three places, and I resolved to attempt the ascent in one of these. On approaching, I found to my satisfaction, a ravine, deeply washed at times by mountain torrents, though now dry, which extended far into the mountain and continually upward. I followed it a long way, not doubting that it would lead me to the summit; but when about half way up the bluffs, this ravine ended in a cave or grot in the side of the mountain very symmetrical and beautiful in its structure, and the walls of which were some twenty to thirty feet in perpendicular height.

Here I found that travelers had cut their names in the soft sandy rock, which formed the sides of the cave, and leaving mine engraved on the wall, I retraced my steps in search of some other mode of ascent. Before descending far, I found one side of the bank not quite so steep, and a possibility indicated of climbing the mountain. At one place there were two or three shelves or projections, looking something like natural steps. I reached one of them and could have attained the second, but saw that the ascent from there was difficult if not impossible.

By winding around the hill side, I arrived at the top of another ravine, which led me by dangerous and difficult paths up and up the mountain, and after a long walk and much exertion, at length reached the summit.

The scene that greeted my astonished vision defies description. Mighty, ragged, rocky crests, silent sentinels, kept watch and ward over the vast solitude.

The melting snows of countless winters had seamed and scarred their sides, as the sun's heat let loose their thundering torrents down their steep decline.

Years may come and go, many things be remembered and forgotten but the grandeur, sublimity and wild beauty of the scene from that mountain peak shall never be forgotten.

To the north and east lay the Platte valley; to the southeast, bluffs on bluffs arose forming a sort of amphitheater of mountains with a court or circular plain in the center. To the northwest, Laramie Peak rose high above the distant plains below, distinctly visible, though about 100 miles away. While wrapt in wondering admiration, I cast my eyes to the southeast and saw that a storm was gathering below the mountain. Peals of thunder shot upwards through the clear air and echoed and reverberated through the mountains.

Vivid lightning shot through the dense, dark cloud and broke the storm-cloud, over the devoted plain below.

The rain poured in torrents and as the sun shone down upon the scene with keen intent he painted the storm cloud, with a lovely rainbow.

Above the clouds, shut off from the world below by a dense black wall, my sensations were novel in the extreme. The scene there beheld was one seldom vouchsafed to mortals.

On returning to camp I found that they had witnessed one of those terrific storms well remembered by all who have ever made the journey overland.

The camp was thoroughly drenched and surprised to hear that I had been high above the storm and untouched by it.

On the 17th of June we reached Ft. Laramie and were courteously and hospitably entertained by Gen. Craig, who is stationed here to protect the stage company and emigrants. We traveled several days with nothing worthy of note befalling us, and again struck the Platte on the 21st inst. near the mouth of Deer Creek.

Sunday in camp has many novel features. Some are washing, some cooking, some cleaning wagons and repairing damages, and in general getting themselves and their belongings in condition for the coming week of travel.

In the evening after all things were ready for the start, we gathered around the blazing camp fire for a little recreation.

Though the days are hot, the evenings are cool and a fire is almost always a cheerful and welcome sight. Miss Julia gave us some fine music and then we all joined in singing some of the good old hymns which are dear to every heart.

The evening was passing in a calm, pleasant manner, when a noise of hoofs was heard, and as we were in the Indian territory every ear was strained to listen.

Presently a lone horseman appeared in sight and was soon ascertained to be a white man.

He had traveled from California alone, having encamped but three nights with emigrants in the whole trip.

He was a good specimen of the genus homo. species Americanus, lively, good natured and intelligent, and fearing nothing that walks. We made him at home, prepared a warm meal for him, after which he sank into a quiet sentimental mood, and as he watched Miss Julia passing to and fro, tears trickled down his bronzed but handsome cheeks, which he hastily brushed aside.

It was evident that he was a man with a heart history, and by a little persuasion from Miss Julia, he was induced to tell his story.

THE TRAVELER'S STORY.

There were, sitting around a cheerful fire one evening, quite a large party of ladies and gentlemen, when Miss Harley proposed that they get up an excursion to the Yosemite Valley. The lady had been in California but a few months. and was very enthusiastic in her praises of the country, the climate and the scenery. We entered into the project with alacrity and arranged to leave San Francisco, at an early day. In pursuance of this agreement, a party of six ladies and six gentlemen left the City, for the Yosemite on the morning of Oct. 10th 1855.

All were in high spirits and enjoyed the ride immensely. Miss Harley was the life of the party. Young, beautiful, highly cultured and exceedingly gifted in conversation, she threw the light of her genius on all surrounding objects and kept her companions constantly in fairy land.

When we arrived at the falls of the Yosemite, her delight knew no bounds. She seemed like one entranced, and bounded from peak to peak with the agility of a young gazelle. I cautioned her often, and said to her "My dear girl, you must not venture so far, you will lose your balance and fall. You must not risk your life, for you are more than life to me." She turned her glorious eyes upon me, and with a smile, said, "Fear not for me, dear friend, the God in whom I trust, will preserve me."

We visited the "Big Trees," "The Bridal Veil," and many other places of interest, and were about making arrangements to return, when Miss Harley expressed a wish to visit some caves which had lately been discovered in the mountain side. Her will was law with us all, and so we went.

Bold and frowning cliffs rose high above us, but climb we must and climb we did, until we reached the caves. We entered one of them and found a beautiful stream running through it in which fish abounded. Bats and owls flitted to and fro, and in peering around we discovered signs of human beings. Consternation seized the whole party. All hastily fled. On reaching a safe place, we discovered that Miss Harley was not with us. We returned with all haste, but alas! too late. She had been captured by the Indians!! When this dreadful fact became apparent, my heart stood still and my tongue was paralized. I stood as one dumb with terror. What should be done! What could be done! We resolved to rescue her. Placing the other ladies in as safe a place as possible, the men of the party hastened in pursuit of the savages. Through ravines and caves, we sought her, through rivers we waded, up mountain crags we climbed, now finding the trail of the Indians and now losing it. The party at length, became disheartened and wanted to give up the search. I said "Gentlemen, you ought to return and protect the ladies under your charge, but I will never give her up while life shall last."

At this their courage revived and they resolved to continue the search and rescue, if possible, the lovely Elinor from those ruthless demons. We had just emerged from a cave when looking up we saw a sight which froze our blood with terror. The lovely girl was on a high projecting cliff separated from us by a wide chasm. She stood in the midst of her savage captors with upturned eyes and hair streaming in the wind. She implored them to spare her, but with fiendish yells they were preparing to torture her. She cast one glance of recognition at us, uttered a piercing cry and threw herself from the cliffs. Utterly powerless to save her, I saw her dashed to pieces on those cruel rocks.

I would have thrown myself over the precipice and died with her had not my friends withheld me. From that moment I died to all that men call happiness."

When the traveler ended, there was not a dry eye in the company, and for some moments there was a profound silence. Respect and sympathy for this afflicted man filled every breast. A mournful smile stole over his features, when at length Miss Julia ventured some words of consolation. He shook his head, "No dear lady, my heart lies buried with her in that deep, dark canon. I wander aimlessly above her, until it shall please the Good Father to call me hence where I hope to be united to her never to part."

CHAPTER VI.

INCIDENTS OF TRAVEL.

Monday, June 16.

We encamped to night near Cold Springs twenty seven miles from Scott's Bluffs. This place has more advantages for settlement than any we have passed since Marysville, Kansas.

Here at least four prominent points attract attention: first, a splendid spring of water, one of the best, purest and most abundant I ever saw: second, a tolerably good soil: third, the Platte River rushing along with its inexhaustible supply of water and its undeveloped capabilities as a carrying stream: fourth, here, for the first time for hundreds of miles, are found trees sufficient in size and number to be dignified by the name of timber. Here it seems a man might find a home and the means of living and here the Great American Desert may be said to end.

Tuesday, June 17.

Arrived at Fort Laramie, and were very courteously and generously treated by Gen. Craig, Commandant. Both at Ft. Kearney and here we were surprised to find no Fort properly speaking, and only a collection of Officers' buildings, Sutler's Store, Post Office and soldiers' tents.

Wednesday, June 18.

Drove to day thirty miles over roads hilly, muddy and sandy by turns and encamped near Horse Shoe Station.

The Ranch here is situated upon a swiftly flowing stream surrounded by hills looming up on all sides, and everything indicates more enterprise than is common in this wild country.

Saturday, June 27.

To day we have again struck the Platte River after having travelled 100 miles since leaving Ft. Laramie. This evening while "standing guard," I heard a rumbling noise which proved to be the banks of the Platte caving in from the action of the River which has a rapid current and here makes a short bend. The Peninsula about thirty rods across will soon be worn away and our present camping ground will be one of those picturesque little islands which abound in the River and which greatly relieve the monotony of that long stretch of country through which the traveler must pass and which is technically called "The Plains."

While passing along the level banks of the Platte we are constantly reminded of the fact that this is one of nature's own road beds and must some day have a Rail-Road which will take passengers over this valley with lightning speed and link the East and West together with bands of steel.

For several days we traveled along with only the usual incidents, crossed the North Platte, paid $5 a team for ferriage and $5 per bu. for grain for our horses and making an average of 25 miles a day. At Sweet Water bridge we found Major Farrell with a company of troops and received supplies which were very timely and acceptable. As we make a turn in the road Independence Rock appears to our astonished eyes. It is a bold and picturesque granite rock rising high above the surrounding bluffs and seems to stand, like a sentinel of liberty, guarding the surrounding plains. We encamped for dinner near its base and some of the party attempted an ascent which however they found a difficult undertaking.

Devil's Gate was the next sensation. We had heard many wild stories about this place and Miss Julia had set her heart on making a pilgrimage to the very spot. Accordingly we encamped early in the afternoon and after a hearty meal, prepared to make the exploration. As we drew near the awful chasm through which the Sweet Water pours its waters, foaming and dashing as if lashed into fury by some unseen power, a sort of wierd and solemn awe crept over us, chilling us to the marrow.

The Professor said that "this was an evidence of one of the greatest convulsions of nature and must have shaken old Mother Earth to her very center." The rocks here seem to be split into two separate ledges as if by a wedge, smooth and perpendicular for hundreds of feet. Miss Julia said afterward that "if this was the entrance to the dominions of his Satanic Majesty, she would prefer to go no further than the gate."

As we were descending into the valley, we saw a little wreath of smoke slowly curling up through the cool air and as this is always a sign of a human habitation in these wild regions, we came upon a hunter's cave, in the side of the rocks. He was preparing his evening meal and was a fine looking half-blood.

The gentleman of the party soon engaged him in conversation and found him very intelligent.

Jean Le Beau, for that was the hunter's name, had been in these regions since boy-hood going only occasionally among civilized men. His father was one of those daring Frenchmen who have done so much to extend the knowledge of the Rocky Mountains. He was a trapper and hunter for many years and was the interpreter for the Indians with the Government. He married a chief's daughter and this son was at home among his mother's people.

We lingered around the mouth of his cave and listened to many exciting stories of adventures and dangers and many legends of surpassing interest.

It was growing late. The shadows were lengthening and a mist was rising over the boiling angry waters as we watched them emerge from the narrow gorge. A nervous shudder seized us as we thought we heard the sound of footsteps near. It was the hunter's wife returning with her baby strapped upon her back. She was more frightened than we, until reassured by a few words in Indian, from her husband.

THE LEGEND OF DEVIL'S GATE.

"Many hundreds of years ago there dwelt in a lovely valley beyond this pass a powerful nation of Indian warriors.

They were brave in battle and knew not fear. Fish and game were plenty and they knew neither cold nor hunger.

They grew rich and powerful and forgot to worship the "Great Spirit" or to offer up sacrifices as they were wont to do. The "Great Spirit" was angry, the earth shook, and the mountains were rent in twain. Many of these people were swallowed up and the mighty river which had made their country a paradise disappeared from their valley forever."

The moon was rising and threw a pale and ghostly light on all the surroundings. We returned to camp feeling that every shrub was an Indian warrior in disguise and found that there was considerable concern among our friends at our lengthened stay.

To-day, Thursday, June 26, we came in sight of the Rocky Mountains proper, looming up in the distance, their snow-crowned summits mingling with the clouds. To one who had never before beheld these frowning sentinels looking down from such vast heights upon this lower earth the sight is grand beyond description. Our company were in high spirits and we enjoyed greatly the change from the monotony of sand, sage brush and grease wood which had been our staple articles of scenery much of the way. We encamped at "Three Crossings" near a Mormon train of ninety five wagons on the way to Omaha to bring in emigrants to Salt Lake.

The train is sent out by "the Church" and the "brethren" are allowed $60 for the use of a yoke of oxen for the trip, which is credited on tithing. "The Church" charges each emigrant $40 passage money, which is to be paid out of his earnings when arriving in the "promised land."

Three hundred wagons are sent to "bring in" five thousand saints. This is the first glimpse we have had of the way "brotherBrigham" financiers.

We are now in the heart of the Indian country and what is strange but well understood in these regions is that we see no Indians. Miss Julia thought she saw one to-day as she was walking a little ahead of the train. When we were among the Pottawatomies, we were a good deal annoyed by the Indians wanting to "swop" with us. Miss Julia had a very bright scarlet scarf which greatly inflamed the cupidity of the young "bucks." One of these young "swells" had a handsome pony which he offered to give for Miss Julia's scarf. She told him she would "swop" and if he would dismount and deliver the pony she would let him have the scarf, but just at the critical moment he would back out and mounting his pony ride away like the wind. In a short time he would be back riding alongside the wagon and saying "swop," "swop," but evidently it was his intention to get hold of the scarf without giving the pony. He followed us a whole day in this way, but when he became satisfied that the "white squaw" was too smart for him he gave it up in disgust.

Miss Julia thought that it was this same scarf

which had attracted the attention of the Indians to-day. We visited an Indian wigwam one day and were introduced to the Princess of the tribe. She was decked out in style. A whole sheet of tin must have been used up in furnishing her bracelets and other adornments. She had a robe of deer-skin elaborately embroidered with beads. Fringe of the same material depended gracefully from the lower parts of the garment. Her face was handsomely decorated with variously colored paints. From her hair hung many species of feathers and bright strips of tin mingled with beads and shells. The ribbons of our ladies fascinated her and she more than hinted that she wanted us to give them to her. In fact she became so urgent upon the subject that we found it to our advantage to take a rather unceremonious leave of "Her Highness."

Saturday, June 28.

We made camp this afternoon rather early, on the mountain side near a snow bank. We are now rising rapidly into a higher region and the atmosphere is truly delightful. The sun is very hot in the middle of the day but the air is cool, coming from the snowy peaks of the Rocky Mountains. This spot is one of nature's loveliest productions. A cool and sparkling spring gushes from the mountain a little above, and spreads out over the lower levels, carpeting them with beautiful green shades ever varying as a cloud flits before the sun, changing the shades as the chameleon ever changes. Below is a level plateau rocky and barren save a few straggling evergreens of stunted growth. In this lovely spot we were resting and preparing the evening meal. The biscuits were baking in the tin oven and the antelope and bacon frying on the stove, and sending up an aroma delicious to inhale. Some one looking down the valley spied a horseman coming towards our camp in hot haste. "The Indians, the Indians," he cried "are upon us. We want twenty of your men to come and help us." Imagine the consternation and confusion. A hasty consultation was had and we decided that it would not do for the men to leave our camp to assist the other, but that we must look to our own safety. The courier reported that his camp about one mile east had been attacked and that two men were killed, that the Indians had gone away but were momentarily expected back and that we must prepare for an attack at any moment.

We hastily prepared to join with other emigrants at a sort of natural fort which we found about one mile distant. We collected about seventy wagons and forming a "corral," with our animals inside, threw up earth works and stationed picket guards about our camp. The men held a meeting, elected officers and made arrangements for an attack. The camp one mile east of us had been attacked and two men killed.

Some valuable stock had also been shot. One noble steed was pierced with many poisoned arrows. We sent a small party to assist in burying the dead. All was now on military footing. The camp was under martial law. No one was allowed to depart or enter without giving the countersign. Sentinels walked upon their beats and were relieved at stated intervals by others. Every ear was strained to hear the war-whoop. No one thought of sleep.

About midnight the camp was startled by the firing of two gun shots not far distant. This was the signal agreed upon with the camp east of us in case they were attacked. For a moment we were sure we heard the wild war-whoop of the savages as they pounced upon their victims. The ladies pale with terrror walked up and down the camp trying to be calm. Miss Julia and Mrs. Burlingame were watching over the children and expecting soon to see the tomahawks of the Indians raised over their heads. "This was a moment of supreme agony" writes Mrs. B. to a friend "as we were certain that it was to be but a few moments of terrible suspense before the dread reality would be upon us."

It was ascertained after a little that the shots were fired by our own men, who were returning from burying their dead friends, and having lost their way fired the usual signal shots in order to have our boys in camp know where they were and answering, enable them to find the camp. With a feeling of infinite relief and devout thankfulness for this danger averted, we laid down to snatch a little rest, not knowing what might yet befall us.

The next day being Sunday, we remained in camp to rest and prepare for future defense.

Story after story came into camp about Indian attacks and outrages and by night we were in a state bordering on distraction. The guard was increased, every weapon made ready, our camp was joined to another in the same locality and every precaution was taken to avoid a surprise. All next day we traveled in solid phalanx with men detailed to guard the advance of the train. Our route lay among mountain fasnesses fit for the haunts of savages. Beautiful springs gushed from the mountain sides flowing down into lovely little valleys forming the most bewitching landscapes and making the weary and way-worn emigrant wish to rest here forever.

But alas, for all things beautiful! These are the very spots where the savages are most likely to fall on their victims. These are their oases in the desert wilderness which surrounds them. Here they repair after the fatigues of hunting and long marches to rest and enjoy their booty. We passed the Stillwater and coming out on to an open prairie we encamped near a beautiful spring.

Tuesday, July 1.

This morning, Messrs. Bradish, Sexton, Manuel and myself rode over to the camp of Col. Collins of the 6th Ohio Cavalry. We had a beautiful ride along the Sweetwater, winding as it here does, in a narrow valley between hills on either side. Making a sudden turn we came at once upon the camp. I applied to Col. Collins for an escort, which was readily granted and thirty men detailed to go with our train to Green River. Thursday, July 3.

We are now on the banks of the famous Green River, the Mississippi of this region. The old Charon who has presided over the ferry here for twenty eight years tells us that it has never been so high before. The banks are overflowed and the water has backed up into the ravines making three rivers instead of one to cross. There are of course no boats to ferry across these bayous and we have to improvise bridges. This is done by cutting trees and throwing them in until a tolerably solid road-way or pontoon bridge is formed. The men then pull the wagons over, as horses would be sure to break through. The horses swim over and are ready to draw the wagons to the next bridge. We had to construct two of these bridges before we were near enough to get to the ferry. We are now all safely over the bayous and on a beautiful little island. The teams and men are very much fatigued and we have concluded to stay here over the 4th of July. We went into camp to-night amid the roar of angry waters all around us and though exposed to dangers on every side we were thankful and fearless and as I write the camp is as quietly sleeping as if in a place of perfect security.

This wild life and constant adventure soon takes away fear and inclines people to be rather reckless. However with our trusty Ohio "boys" we feel no fear of Indians. The danger is from a sudden and rapid rise in the river which would place us in a very perilous position.

From Miss Julia's Journal.

Thursday, July 3.

The perils and hair breadth escapes of the past week will never be erased from my memory.

Oh! if we could have foreseen all the trials,

difficulties, and dangers of this over-land journey we should never have left our comfortable homes for the sake of adventure. When the gentlemen who rode over to camp left us we feared it would be a final leave. They were going through the worst Indian country, a region strewn with the bones of emigrants who had fallen by the tomahawks of the savages.

When, yesterday, they returned and with them came thirty five stalwart Ohio volunteers, there was great rejoicing and three rousing cheers greeted the soldiers. I must close my journal to prepare for to-morrow's festivities, as we are going to celebrate the 4th of July on the "Plains."

Friday, July 4th.

As the sun rose he was greeted by a volley of musketry which continued at intervals until the camp was all astir. It had been decided that we were to have a 4th of July oration, so a speaker's stand was erected under the spreading trees of the Island and the venerable orator of the day Judge Drave took his seat on the platform, the band struck up "Hail Columbia" and our little party soon assembled to listen to a most excellent and patriotic discourse. He alluded in most feeling terms to the war raging between the North and South and deprecated the shedding of fratricidal blood. "But" said he, "the Union must and shall be preserved at any and all hazards." "North, South, East and West, all parts of our common country, bound together by ties of blood, language and religion, may they ever remain as now one undivided Republic." Loud applause greeted the speaker as he descended from the rustic stage. The party now divided as seemed most congenial. Some played football, others chess or eucher while the younger portion selected a beautiful green lawn and danced to the merry music of the band.

The ladies being greatly in the minority many of the gentlemen selected partners from their comrades tying a handkerchief around their arms to distinguish them. I never saw a merrier or more orderly party. But everything must come to an end, so the dancers, the ball players, the chess and card players all gathered round a sumptuous repast.

In mirth and hilarity, sallies of wit and pungent jokes, after dinner toasts and stories of adventure, the day wore away. All concurred in saying that it had been a most delightful one. Evening drew on and as is customary in this region a bright camp fire was built and all gathered round. We had heard much of the tactics of the Indians in warfare and so insisted that Sergeant Ellston should relate some of his experi-

THE SERGEANT'S STORY. 57

ences with the treacherous savages. "We started" said he "one fine morning in pursuit of a band of hostile braves. We knew that they were in our immediate vicinity. We also knew that they had their squaws and luggage with them, encamped on the banks of the Sweet Water.

We thought we had a "dead sure thing" on them and so pressed on in fine spirits. The river at this point was not fordable and there was no ferry. We felt sure we should surprise them and that being unable to get across the river they would fall an easy prey. They had been very troublesome to the emigrants and had killed and robbed many families, while crossing the plains. Imagine our surprise and chagrin when on arriving at the river we found their camp deserted and no trace either up or down the river could we find. How could they have escaped? In our search we found the cabin of an old mountaineer and learned from him how they had escaped. He said that fearing the approach of the troops the Indians had the day before all gone over the river and could now be seen on the other side preparing for a long march. The squaws papooses and luggage had been sent over in bark canoes and the horses and braves swam the river. This was a most difficult feat and one utterly beyond the reach of our soldiers. An Indian will send in his pony, strap his blanket and musket on the top of his head, plunge in after the pony and thus swim almost any river. "It took us three days" said the Sergeant "to build a bridge that we dare trust to carry us across and by this time the Indians were far beyond our reach, resting and recruiting, in some lovely valley in security." "These savages" continued he "are perfectly familiar with all this country while our boys are total strangers. Every cave, mountain, river and valley, are alike easy of access to them and while our troops are planning how they can reach any point, the Indians are there by some short cut or secret mountain pass, long before them. It is almost impossible to dislodge them or do anything with them on their own hunting grounds."

At the request of Sergeant Ellston I brought out my Guitar and we sang some parting songs. The "boys" leave us to-morrow, as Green River is as far as Col. Collin's command goes. We feel deeply grateful for their protection and shall long remember this 4th of July on the Green River Island. All joined in singing "Home, Sweet Home," and at its close, retired to rest, to be prepared for the excitements and fatigues of the coming day.

CHAPTER VII.
CLOSING SCENES AND TRIALS.

From Mr. Burlingame's Journal.
                    Saturday, July 5.

We arose this morning, feeling that we had a "Big Job," as Lincoln calls the Rebellion, before us. We had crossed two sloughs preliminary to the main crossing and had now to cross the third to get to the ferry. We drove in our four horses and in a twinkling the strong current took them off their feet. They were all down and I was in the water trying to get the harness off them leaving them free to swim. As I was on the upper side of the wagon the current carried me under the horses feet. One of the horses lost all heart and would have drowned had not her head been held out of the water. In this plight myself and all the horses must have perished had not Mrs. B. induced some men, total strangers to us, to risk their lives to save mine. They swam in and assisting the horses to their feet, adjusted the harness and let the horses free from the wagons, when they swam to the opposite bank in safety. Then by means of long ropes fixed to the wagon we managed to pull it through. We were now at the ferry but standing in three feet of water. By this time many were waiting to cross and we stood there waiting our turn until nearly dark. The ferry was a flat scow large enough for two wagons and several horses, and was propelled by a rope. To cross on such a boat over such a wide and swift stream would be risking a good deal, but to cross now when the mountain snows had swollen this to a tremendous flood, roaring like a cataract was dangerous in the extreme. There was however no help for it and we had to nerve ourselves to the task. Just as it became our turn to cross and the shades of night made everything appear more portentous we looked up the stream and beheld with dismay an immense tree with huge branches washing down upon our ferry. We held our breath. Would the branches catch the rope and break it and thus leave us here, we knew not how long? Would the tree ride under the rope. We strained our eyes to see. The huge monster, heedless of our presence or our needs rushed on. The top branches caught the rope, passed it and left it whole. Hurrah for the rope, hurrah for the rope, hip, hip, hurrah!! We are safe. God be thanked was devoutly breathed by many voices. On we drove with our household goods, trusting to this frail bark which quivered and creaked in every joint. As we neared the powerful and swift current we momentarily expected to be swallowed up. A single move of the horses or any change in the ba'ance would have been fatal. The horses understood the danger as well as we and kept perfectly quiet until we were safe against the other shore. This the crowning peril of our perilous journey being safely passed, we went into camp with grateful hearts.

Monday, July 7.

At Green River we took a new escort of six mounted men, Mormon volunteers. We traveled yesterday about 18 miles and encamping at Ham's Fork, formed the acquaintance of Judge Carter and lady of Ft. Bridger. They were en route for the States. . Judge C. gave us letters of introduction to Mr. Hamilton and Col. Mann of Ft. Bridger. On arriving at Bridger to-day, we were most kindly received and hospitably entertained by the resident officers and men. Bridger is a perfect gem on these arid plains, an oasis in the desert. Every thing that generous hearts could devise was done to make our stay here delightful. We were invited to Judge Carter's residence and entertained in right royal style by Mr. Hamilton who had charge in the absence of the Judge.

The drive yesterday, over rough roads at a rapid rate, and our long drive to-day have so wearied our horses that I determined to leave them at the Ft. and go on by stage. The Mormon escort to-day put their own horses in our wagon and let ours rest. Sergeant Atwood has volunteered to procure for us four fresh mules to take us on to Salt Lake City. This offer was gratefully accepted.

Tuesday, July 8.

This morning, Sergeant Atwood appeared with the mules and a new escort of six mounted men, and about ten o'clock we started under more favorable auspices for Salt Lake City. Not wishing to leave the train with which we had traveled so long, we delayed starting and traveled as slowly as we could induce the "boys" to go, but the escort was composed of young mormons who had been in the volunteer service against the Indians and having been out two months, were in a hurry to get home. However we managed to stop them in "Quaking Asp Hollow," twenty eight miles from the Ft. and our friends coming

NEEDLE ROCK. 63

up we all made camp together. The grass tonight was very fine, with plenty of sage-wood for fuel and tolerably good water. On the whole this is a very good camp and as I am relieved from the care of my five horses, which were left at Ft. B. I am in a good situation to enjoy the pleasures of camp life. I retired feeling better than any time since leaving the States. The face of the country has undergone a wonderful change. The country is rough and mountainous, but vegetation begins to appear. Something besides the everlasting sage brush and grease wood so often mentioned by Horace Greely in his "Trip to California and Oregon." At Quaking Asp Spring, there is a beautiful grove of these trees, rising tier above tier and making a very lovely and attractive picture, breaking upon the sight suddenly after seeing nothing of the kind for nearly a thousand miles. We are now approaching Salt Lake Valley, and we all share in the feeling of delight incident to getting to our journey's end. We crossed Bear River on a toll bridge and charged the toll to "Uncle Sam." We encamped for our nooning yesterday at Needle Rock one of the most picturesque bits of scenery on our way. The rocks rise up in spires like huge needles and seem to be made literally of steel, they glisten so in the sunlight. The needles are of all lengths and some seem to pierce the sky. A cool refreshing stream flows down the canon making the sweetest music that weary travelers in these regions can ever hear. In the afternoon we had a delightful ride down Echo Canon. This is a beautiful valley twenty five or thirty miles long and so named because of the position of the mountains in which sound reverberates from side to side in a most wonderful manner filling the valley with goblins, fairies, demons and all sorts of wierd and unearthly sounds.

Our mormon drivers are very Jehus and the way we drove down those steep and dangerous declivities, turning sharp corners and dashing over rocks and streams, was something fearful to contemplate. We passed Cache Cave a large opening in the solid rock and our guides regaled us with many wild adventures with Indians and Road Agents who had their rendezvous in this cave. Our escort were also detailed to take two prisoners, horse thieves, to Salt Lake City. We were surprised to see them allowed full liberty to go where they pleased and upon inquiry we were told that this was the custom in this country, Brigham Young's plan being to give the prisoners every chance to escape and then to have them shot down by the police, thus saving considerable expense. Our delinquents understood the game perfectly and made not the slightest effort to leave us. We were now within a few miles of 'Zion.'

Between the western border of the States on the Atlantic side, and the Pacific States, there are vast prairies, dreary and treeless, sand-hills, mud-flats, rocky mountains and rapid rivers. After a journey of twelve hundred miles, winding through the tortuous mountain defiles, crossing rivers with precipitous banks and rushing, mighty currents, over roads that would terrify expert Jehus, wearied with a monotony of sand, sage brush and grease wood, we stand at last on an eminence of the Wahsatch Mountains, over eight thousand feet above the level of the Ocean, surrounded by peaks that rise majestically above our heads, and in the deep nooks of which continually glitters eternal snow. Behind us are receding hills, streams sparkling like diamonds in the sunlight, the trembling foliage of the quaking aspen, narrow gorges and dark, deep abysses in the distance. Before us, the mountains grow lower, and a lovely valley relieves the sight in the south west. This is our first glimpse of the Valley of the Great Salt Lake. Here on the summit of "big mountain," the mormon em.grants fall on their knees and pray; some shout hosannas and hallelujahs; many weep; husbands kiss their wives, and parents their children in their joy, and the very faithful declare that they feel the Spirit of God pervading the atmosphere and enthusiastically believe all their toils fully repaid, for they have at length come home, where the "wicked cease from troubling and the weary are at rest." We felt almost as happy as the mormons, to know that our long and perilous journey was at an end and that only eighteen miles now separated us from rest and society.

Sergeant Atwood, a chivalric Englishman, was greatly elated with his position and was determined to go into Salt Lake City in grand style. Accordingly on the morning of the day we were to reach the City, he called his escort together and detailed two to ride ahead, two behind and one on each side of the wagon in the fashion of the retainers of the middle ages. The cortege thus arranged, we cross another mountain ridge, and descend into a most delightfully picturesque gorge, the "Emigration Canon." Admiring the beauties of its rocky heights, the slopes covered with shrubbery and painted in all sorts of rich colors, as though a rainbow had been wrecked on the hillside, we turn an abrupt point and the sight that greets our eyes, is indeed beautiful.

The valley lies spread out like a green pasture,

SALT LAKE CITY.

the Jordan like a thread of silver winding through, the golden grain waving in the wind, the orchards with their ruddy fruit, the gardens filled with vegetables and sweet scented flowers, all give evidence that the Goddess of plenty presides over this lovely valley of the Saints.

We are on the rolling brow of a slight decline, several hundred feet above our heads there are long, level lines of ridges, which are deeply indented on the mountains, as far as our sight can reach. These are called "benches," and extend throughout the entire range of valleys; are plainly visible, exactly level, and are the ancient shores of the Great Salt Lake, which lies like a blue tinted mirror 35 miles to the north-west. As we drove down these plateaus or benches, that rise one above another, the bugler made the welkin ring with his merry notes, the inhabitants, men women and children rushed to the streets to see us ride by. Thus heralded we drew up at the "Townsend House" and were very graciously received by "mine host."

CHAPTER VIII.

LIFE AMONG THE MORMONS.

The news spread rapidly and soon all Salt Lake City knew that the Judges had arrived and that they had brought their families, and had come to live among them. Gov. H. was here, having arrived a few days before. All mormondom was on the qui vive. We received numerous calls and invitations, boquets, and baskets of fruit, and every attention that we could desire. Mrs. Hooper, wife of the mormon representative in congress, called and invited us to her house for the following day. We met a number of prominent mormons as well as several "gentile" merchants. Miss Julia was delighted with Mrs. H. and declared that she could see no difference between mormons and other people. In a few days it was intimated than President Young would be happy to receive a call from the Judges and families. His Highness never makes calls, but is always called upon, a la the crowned heads of Europe. Judge Drave, Mrs. Burlingame, Miss Julia and myself, called on "President Young" and were very graciously received. Brigham Young is a man of medium height, compact frame, with a manner deliberate and impressive. His hair is sandy and inclined to curl, features regular and expressive of great determination. The lower jaw is firmly set and very heavy, indicating a savage vindictiveness, which one would dislike to arouse. His manner towards strangers is simple and unpretending, almost winning. In conversation he is pleasant and affable, but under the slightest contradiction or opposition, he becomes restive, his eye flashes fire and the savage element predominates at once. Strangers are favorably impressed with the first visit to his office. They go to see and hear and Brigham looks well and is a good talker. He has talent, if not genius, when therefore, he is master of the field and has the choice of topics, he never fails to make himself interesting.

Our call was very pleasant. He invited the ladies to call again, when he would introduce them to "some of his wives," and have "some of his daughters" play for them. He was very polite to Miss Julia telling her he knew she would like the city and the people, and hoping her stay with "his people," would prove agreeable.

Yesterday, Sunday, we all attended church at the tabernacle. Temple Square contains ten acres; surrounded by a ten-foot wall, with four gates, around which are planted some shade trees. We enter at the South gate and to the west is the tabernacle. This is an adobe structure 126 feet long by 64 feet wide. It will seat over 2000 persons and it is here that Brigham and other leaders give the word of the Lord every sabbath to the people. There is an instrumental band that plays marches, polkas, original mormon songs to the tune of "old Dan Tucker," Bach's chants and Haendel's oratorios. A fine organ and good choir also add to this unique entertainment. Upon our entrance we were immediately shown to one of "Bro. Brigham's" pews and seated with Mrs. Cobb one of the most accomplished of his wives. In the course of the sermon Brigham said

"I defy the world to prove that I have infringed upon the United States law. If you tell them a mormon has two wives they are shocked and call it blasphemy. If you whisper such a thing in the ears of a gentile, who takes a fresh wife every night he is thunderstruck with the enormity of the crime.

"When the officers returned from this territory to the states, did we send them away? We did not. I will tell you what I did and what I will do again. I did chastise the poor, mean, miserable ruffian, the poor, miserable creature who came here, b. the name of Brochus, when he arose before this people, to preach to them, and tell them of meanness which he supposed they were guilty of and traduce their character. It is true, as it is said in the report of these officers, if I had crooked my little finger he would have been used up. But I did not bend it. If I had, the sisters alone felt indignant enough to have chopped him in pieces."

This and more of the same sort made up the sermon which was evidently intended for the benefit of the new federal officers who were all present. Thus forewarned, the Governor and Judges, resolved to proceed carefully and to avoid any conflict with the mormon authorities, if possible. In a few days we received an invitation to tea at the house of Mrs. Cook.

Several of our party had known this lady in the States. She and her husband were on their way to California, and on arriving at Salt Lake City were so pleased with the place and people, that they concluded to remain. Mrs. C. being a fine musician was soon interested in the choir and singing societies and was so handsomely and generously treated by Young that she embraced the faith. She is a prominent person in mormon society, and it is at her home that "Bro. Brigham" meets those gentiles whom he wishes to influence. Miss Julia was quite elated, feeling that we were about to meet with some of the elite of mormondom. We met here President Brigham Young and Mrs. Cobb, one of his most accomplished wives, Secretary Fuller, several mormon dignitaries and their wives, Mr. and Mrs. Bradish, Professor Redfield, Gov. Harding and Judge Drave. The prophet was politeness itself, and introduced us to all of the company, and conversed in a most animated and agreeable manner. He was particularly amiable and gallant to Miss Julia. During the course of the evening, the conversation turned on the change of Governor, and Judges, and Brigham's brow darkened at once and he said: "There is no need of any difficulty, and there need be none if the officers do their duty and mind their own affairs. If they do not, if they undertake to interfere in affairs that do not concern them, I will not be far off. There was Almon W. Babbitt. He undertook to quarrel with me, but soon afterwards was killed by the Indians. He lived like a fool and died like a fool."

Thus at the very outset, we were in a most pointed and significant manner warned against in any way interfering with the peculiar institutions of the "Saints." Under the guise of politeness and friendship, we could plainly see the dark and villainous character of the man with whom we had to deal.

CHAPTER IX.

LIFE AMONG THE MORMONS.

We arrived in Salt Lake City on the 11th of July, and the 24th is the anniversary of Mormon Independence. The Mormons keep this day and celebrate it as we do the 4th of July. Great preparations were in progress throughout the City. The Governor and Judges were invited to join in the procession and they and their families to attend the grand ball in the evening.

It is the policy of the Mormon leaders to keep the people amused and hence dancing and parties are very frequent and popular. This annual ball, however, is the event of the season and only the *ton* can hope to attend it.

We had great expectations and were preparing to see Mormon society at its best. The evening came and we repaired to the great Hall. It was a scene of gayety indeed, the Prophet and his wives, the "Heads" of the church and their wives in brilliant array were there and "all went merry as a marriage bell." Governor Harding, the new Judges and their ladies were given seats of honor and the eyes of all were upon them. The introductions were truly a novelty. The high dignitaries introduced their wives to us several in succession. After this unique ceremony, Governor H. said to one of the ladies as he led her forth to the dance, "The President has introduced several of his wives to me as 'Mrs. Young,' 'Mrs. Young,' 'Mrs. Young.' As well might the astronomer point me to the stars in the heavens, without giving me their names." "Governor, I understand your compliment and appreciate it. The name of this particular Star is Lucy." Judge Burlingame having invited "Mrs. Young" to dance, "President" Young turned to Mrs. Burlingame and said, "You see your husband there dancing with one of my wives, will you accept me as a partner for the next set?" Mrs. Burlingame said, "President Young, I do not dance." He took a seat by her side and said, "Will you allow your husband to dance when you do not?" She said, "Certainly, I do what I think is right, and he does the same. "I have no wish to dictate to him and he does not dictate to me." "Ah," said he, "This is new doctrine, right is but a relative term, the circumstances must determine that." The set ended and the Prophet, gay and smiling, with great suavity and politeness addressed Miss Julia and invited her for the next dance.

He was faultlessly attired and a good dancer and as he led the beautiful Gentile lady forth, all eyes were turned that way, and no doubt many a jealous pang racked many a heart.

The balls afford splendid opportunities to the men for flirting with the girls. No matter how old or how homely a man is, he thinks he has as much right to flirt and dance with the girls as the youngest boy; for they all consider themselves single men if they have a dozen wives. Every young woman that comes among these people, is courted and flattered by the old married men as much or more, as by the young men. Miss Julia was the admired of all admirers.

The President had set the example and the other dignitaries vied with each other in doing her homage. She was affable and gracious and treated all in a very charming manner.

The ladies were equally pleased and she made

many acquaintances among the "plural" wives. As she was sitting quietly conversing with an army officer, she over-heard two Mormon women talking. One said, "My husband has brought his girl here to-night; but I have not spoken to her and I don't intend to. See her" she exclaimed, "making love to him and smiling so sweetly. I could tear her in pieces."

Thus suddenly was disclosed to Miss Julia the horrible nature of Polygamy. While all were smiles and gayety on the surface, underneath were the monsters of jealousy, hatred and revenge. Just at this juncture, supper was announced.

President Young escorted Mrs. Burlingame, Judge Burlingame invited Mrs. Emeline Free Young. Governor Harding, Mrs. Lucy Bigelow Young, and General Kimball accompanied Miss Julia. The meal was elegant, the dishes abundant and well served. After dinner speeches, toasts, wit and repartee combined to make the "feast of reason and flow of soul" complete.

After supper the guests returned to the ball room and tripped the "light fantastic toe" until the morning hours.

During the evening many odd and laughable incidents occurred. Heber C. Kimball introduced five or six of his wives to us in succession, and when asked if these were all, replied, "O dear! no, I have a few more at home and fifty or so scattered over the earth somewhere."

We left the Hall about 2 A. M. having witnessed the most novel and interesting scene of our lives.

All this time we had been boarding at the "Townsend House," and we now were obliged to turn our attention to the more disagreeable pastime of house-hunting. We soon found that all the property here is consecrated to the Church and that we could not even rent a house without consulting Brigham Young. We found a house formerly occupied by Judge Stiles which could be had if Bro. Brigham was willing, so a correspondence was opened with the Prophet and he graciously consented that we should have the house.

We now addressed ourselves to getting settled and were kindly assisted by our neighbors who were all polygamists. One family across the way consisted of three sisters, all married to one man. Our landlord had two wives, one we could understand, the other we could not. They were good neighbors, called us Brother and Sister and brought us of their poultry, fruits and vegetables and received in exchange what they rarely tasted, tea, coffee and sugar.

As soon as we were settled, we began to look about us and use our eyes and ears. What we saw and heard did not incline us to retain the favorable opinion we had formed of Mormon society.

We soon found that the people were under an absolute despotism, and that their lives and liberties were wholly in the power of one man. Nothing could be said or done, no business transacted without his knowledge or consent. During what is called the reformation, all the people were required to make deeds of their homes and place them *in trust* in Brigham's hands. Thus they were body and soul in his power and if they varied from his will in any way, their houses and lands were forfeited to the Church.

Miss Julia had written some very interesting and spicy letters to the Boston papers in which she had criticised polygamy in an unfriendly manner. This changed their whole course towards us from the kindest consideration, to the bitterest hostility.

We were all attending Church one Sunday at the Tabernacle, when we were surprised and startled to hear ourselves denounced by Heber C. Kimball, 1st Counsellor to Brigham, in the following language. "These are d—d pretty ladies and gentlemen to come here among us and after being treated to the best we have, to denounce our Institutions and abuse our hospitality. If I had my way I would send them to h—ll cross lots, and I now in the name of Israel's God, curse them, from the crowns of their heads to the soles of their feet, henceforth and forever." From this time everything was done to annoy and intimidate us.

The Judges and Governor were openly threatened on the public streets. Miss Julia seeing what a storm she had innocently raised, was greatly alarmed, and a good opportunity offering she left Salt Lake City, and took up her residence in Carson City, Nevada. Mrs. Burlingame was at this time the only "Gentile lady" in Salt Lake City. Notwithstanding the anger of the Mormon leaders, many of the "plural" women came secretly to the house of Mrs. Burlingame and told her their trials and how they disliked polygamy and how happy they would be were they safely out of it.

One very intelligent English woman said she knew polygamy was wrong and wanted to get out of it, but that she dared not make a move as she knew her husband would shoot any man who should assist her or ever afterwards give her any attention. Her story revealed some of the most diabolical features of the Mormon faith, and is as follows:—

"We were living quietly in our lovely cottage home in the outskirts of London and were as happy as husband and wife could be. Our honey moon was scarcely over, when my husband came home one day greatly excited. He told me that some missionaries had arrived from America who brought the most glorious tidings. The new Dispensation was begun on earth and the Millenium was about to be ushered in. The Missionaries had come from the New Jerusalem let down from God out of Heaven, upon the tops of mountains and that all nations were commanded to "flow unto it."

I thought my husband perfect and believed, because he did. We were told that there was neither cold nor hunger in the new City, but that all was peace and joy. We embraced the faith and were soon on our way to "Zion."

Just before leaving England, my husband was ordained an Elder and his faith and enthusiasm knew no bounds. Many things transpired on the long and dreadful journey to sorely shake our faith but we were so blind! So blind!! We were commanded to make the journey overland from Council Bluffs with hand carts, as a trial of our faith and promised a greater exaltation in the next world, as our reward.

In our company there were many wealthy and intelligent ladies who had left all for the new religion. Their money and fine clothing and jewelry had been given to the Church and they had subjected themselves to all the rigors of the inclement season with nothing but the barest necessaries of life. We arrived at the frontier very late and before we had proceeded far on our way, snow began to fall and the weather being very severe, many became sick from want and exposure. We were required to make the journey on foot, in the main, but were sometimes allowed to ride in order to rest our weary frames.

When a river was to be crossed, we were driven into the water, men, women and children, and were told that if our faith was sufficient, we should, like the Israelites of old, go over dry shod. Many men carried their wives and children over as long as they were able. If any were unable to drag their carts, they were obliged to lighten them by throwing away clothing, cooking utensils and even provisions, thus depriving themselves of a certain portion of their daily allowance. Fuel was scarce, and it was often necessary to go into the snow waist deep to procure it. Mr. Chapman, a strong, athletic man, formerly a member of the Queen's Guards, from constant exertion and exposure, at length fell sick.

He was not allowed to ride as long as he could stand and drag one foot before the other. He grew rapidly worse, and it soon became evident that he must die. One morning, when the train was ready to start, the Captain came to the tent of the sick man, and finding him dying, said to Mrs. Chapman, "Your husband must die; leave him in the hands of God and proceed on your journey." "What!" said the heart stricken woman, "leave my husband on this barren waste, a prey to the wolves? No; while there is breath in my body, I shall remain by his side and share his fate. Leave us if you will, for the wild beasts of the desert cannot be more cruel than you have been."

In five minutes more he breathed his last; and throwing him into a hole dug in the sand, they dragged the weeping wife and children from all they held dear on earth. In a few days the same woman left her baby, too, on the sands of the desert, a prey to wolves. She says, "I never can see Franklin D. Richards, (Captain) but I feel hand carts from the crown of my head to the soles of my feet."

Much cruelty was exercised for the slightest disobedience. One young man was whipped nearly to death, merely because he was unable to travel as fast as desired and drag as much on his hand cart as the Captain had given him. Another man who had given up all his money and a valuable gold watch and chain, asked for a dollar back to buy tobacco and was refused. While the men were shamefully treated and abused, many of the younger and better looking women were allowed to ride all the time and to have all they desired to eat, thus depriving the hard working men of their portion.

One day, as we approached our Mecca, an old white-haired saint said to the Captain, in a weak voice, "Captain, I feel as if I should die, drawing in this hand cart. Can't I ride a little while?" "Draw till you die then" replied the hard-hearted wretch, "for I'll be d—d if you can ride."

"Oh, well," said the old man, "I suppose I must draw till I die." He took out his watch. "A quarter of four. It will soon be over. Ten minutes. Oh dear; Oh, my God! Five minutes to four;—four; and the old man fell down in his place,—he was dead."

Every day witnessed the death of large numbers by cold and starvation. Those who survived, were more like walking skeletons than human beings. They were covered with vermin and loathsome to behold. Some were so badly frozen that the flesh fell from their bones.

During all this long and terrible journey, my husband had kept up. He had ministered to the sick and dying, had helped to bear the burdens of the weak, and had in every way shown himself a worthy disciple of the meek and lowly Jesus whose minister he was. He had never heard of the dark and mysterious doctrines of the Church and had only seen the fair and comely garments of the bride of Christ, until he started on this overland journey. When well away from civilization, and so far that return was impossible, the peculiar doctrines began to be darkly hinted at.

We were seated one evening, after a rather easy day, around a camp fire and recalling home and friends, and having a little social chat, when Bro. Richards seated himself in our midst and said, "Brethren and Sisters, there are many things in our blessed religion, which we do not teach among the ungodly Gentiles. If you are faithful, you will soon be ushered into the holy of holies and be permitted to know the mysteries of Godliness, and participate in all the privileges of the Saints of the Most High. Our religion teaches us that there are many Gods, and they are of both sexes. But to us, there is but one God, the Father of mankind, and the Creator of the earth. Men and women are literally, the sons and daughters of God, our spirits having been literally begotten by God, in the heavenly world, and having been afterwards sent to this earth, and invested with these tabernacles. God is in the form of man.

He has a body composed of spiritual matter. There is no difference between matter and spirit, except in quality. Spirit is matter refined.

God is omnipotent, but not personally omnipresent. He is everywhere present by his Holy Spirit. His personality is generally expressed by the phrase, "He has body, parts, and passions." He resides in the center of the universe near the planet Kolob. This planet rotates on its axis once in a thousand of our years, and one revolution of Kolob is a day to the Almighty. Jesus Christ was the Son of God, literally begotten by the Father, and had the Spirit of God in the body of a man.

After his resurrection, he had a body of flesh and bones only, typical of man's resurrected body. He differs in nothing from the Father, except in age and authority,—the Father having the seniority, and consequently the right to preside. The Holy Spirit is a subtle fluid, like electricity. It is the subtlest form of matter and pervades all space. By its agency, all miracles are performed. Miracles are simply the effects of the operation of natural laws. But they are laws of a higher character than those with which we are acquainted.

The Holy Spirit is communicated by the laying on of hands by one of the properly authorized priest-hood, and the recipient is then enabled to perform wonderful things, according to his gift,—some having the gift of prophecy, some of healing, some of speaking in unknown tongues, &c. There are three heavens,—the telestial, the terrestrial and the celestial. The celestial and terrestrial heavens are to be occupied by the various classes of persons who have neither obeyed nor rejected the gospel. The telestial is typified by the Stars,—the terrestrial by the Moon.

The celestial, or highest heaven, has for its type the Sun, and is reserved for those who receive the testimony of Jesus, and were baptized by one having authority from Him, and who afterwards lived a holy life.

The earth, as purified and refined, after the second coming of Christ, is to be the final abode of those entitled to the glories of the celestial kingdom. Jerusalem, is to be rebuilt, and Zion, or the New Jerusalem, is to be built in Jackson County, Missouri, whence the Saints were expelled in 1833.

There is a fourth class of persons, not entitled to either of these heavens. They are those who sin against the Holy Ghost; that is, who apostatize after receiving the Holy Spirit. These go into everlasting punishment, to remain with the devil and his angels. The gospel which men are called upon to obey, in order to gain a place in the Celestial Kingdom, is First,—They must believe in Jesus Christ as the Son of God, in His authorized priesthood, and in His Prophets, Joseph Smith and Brigham Young, Secondly,—They must repent of their Sins; Thirdly,—They must be baptized by immersion for the remission of their own sins and for the sins of their ancestors and families, who died without faith.

Fourthly,—They must receive the laying on of hands for the gift of the Holy Ghost.

Fifthly,—They must believe that there are sins that men commit that cannot be atoned for in this world and that only blood atonement will save their souls. They must have their blood shed by the proper authorities to wit the priesthood, that the smoke thereof may ascend and that the incense may come up before God as an atonement for their sins. Sixthly,—They must believe that if a man is faithful, God will give unto him many wives and concubines as he did unto David and Solomon of old according to the revelation

which God give to His servant Joseph Smith.—
SEVENTHLY,—They must believe that if a man
dies his brother must take his wife and raise up
seed unto his dead brother. Brethren and sisters
these are a few of the principles of our religion
which you will know and understand better when
you have taken your endowments and been sealed
up unto eternal lives.

At the conclusion of this discourse all sat as
if turned to stone. No one ventured to speak.

This horrible revelation in this desert wilderness far from the habitations of men, had something so unearthly and startling in it that we were nigh paralized. I little thought that I was soon to experience the working of one of the most repulsive of these doctrines. After this my husband lost heart; he would remain hours without speaking, he had no appetite and a fever began to burn in his veins.

A few days later we arrived in Salt Lake City the end of our journey, the Mecca of our hopes and plans. My husband grew rapidly worse and the end came, but I was not prepared. I thought he could not die and leave me thus in a strange land. He had a brother but I hated him.

It was late at night, when my husband drew his last breath in my arms. I laid his dear head back on the pillow and as I did so my senses failed.

How long I remained thus, I know not, but when I regained consciousness, I saw bending over me that hated form. His attentions were persistent and unmistakeable; I groaned in spirit and tried to put him from me. He said, "Why resist, you know I have always adored you and now you are mine by our holy religion. I must raise up seed for my dead brother and you must be sealed to your husband while I act as proxy.

"There lies your darling husband. You have never been sealed to him. You have not taken your endowments and if you do not you will not be his in another world."

Oh! the agony of that moment; no words can portray my feelings when I realized that he said the truth. I sent for Brigham Young. I told him how I loved my husband and hated my husband's brother. I besought him to let this cup pass from me. He seemed greatly affected and said I should not be my brother's wife but that he should only act as proxy for my husband in going through the endowment ceremonies which were indispensable in order that I should belong to my husband in another world.

I believed him and as well as I could prepared for the ceremonies. The Priests and Prophets gathered around the dead form of my loved one and the rites for the dead and living were solemnly performed. I was almost insensible to what was passing and only knew that I was being married to my dead.

We laid him to rest, but scarcely had the grave closed its portals, before the hated form of his brother presented itself. I bade him leave me never to return. He smiled a triumphant and wicked smile and said "No, No, my darling, I shall never leave you, for you are my lawfully wedded wife." I had been married to this man over the body of my dead husband. I screamed for help, I invoked the spirit of my dead husband, Bro. Brigham and God himself to free me from this hated bond. My reason fled, for days I lay in a fearful fever and my life hung in the balance.

I sent for Bro. Brigham and told him I could not, would not live if he persisted in making me the wife of the man I hated. At length overcome by my entreaties he gave me a divorce and life began again to seem worth having. I never think of this time without shuddering at the awful fate which I so fortunately escaped."

CHAPTER X.

JOURNEY TO CARSON CITY.

It was a lovely morning in September, 1862, when a coach and four dashed rapidly up in front of the Burlingame residence. Miss Julia, dressed in traveling costume came out and shaking the dust of the Saintly City from her feet was off in search of further adventures. Her traveling companions were Gov. Doty, Supt. of Indian Affairs and Mr. Cook, the manager of the Overland Stage Company. We will let her give us an account of her journey.

"I had been in Salt Lake City about two months and had made the acquaintance of Brigham Young and several of his wives and daughters. I had met most of the principal Apostles and High Dignitaries and had been very handsomely treated until I had in my letters home said something derogatory to the peculiar institution. From this time my stay became very unpleasant and I concluded to go to Nevada. I was sorry to leave my brother and his family behind but considered it my duty to get away while I had a good opportunity.

The only mode of travel being by stage the journey was a difficult and tedious one. Gov. Doty had been many years in the west and entertained us with stories of his travels and hair breadth escapes among the Indians of these mountains. The Snakes and Bannocks had become very hostile and it was necessary to take a trip among them to quiet them down. We started from Salt Lake in May and traveled Northward to Snake River. The Indians in these regions are nearly all Mormons and have their endowment robes. We had a Mormon guide and through him the Indians understood that Brigham wanted them to be friendly.

We called a council of braves and made presents to our Lamanite brethren. They received our presents with condescension. We gave a blanket to one sister, which she received with dignified indifference but when we offered her some vermilion paint, her features became animated and she received it, radiant with smiles.

In fifteen minutes her comely face was bedaubed with it and her beauty greatly heightened in her own estimation. After the treaty was concluded we wound up with an Indian war dance.

On a slight elevation sat the Chiefs and Medicine men, dressed in their robes of state. All the ornamentation known to savage men was brought into use. War paint, beads, shells, bones of animals and fishes, deerskin ornamented with beads and moccasins of the finest. The braves formed a ring around their head men and the musicians with bones, rude drums and a sort of triangle, began the march. Round and round they circled, growing more and more excited with the exercise and noise until the very heavens were rent with their fiendish yells and cries.

Ever and anon they would set up the war-whoop and then all would join hands and suddenly fall prostrate on the ground. We were only too happy when the ball broke up and gladly escaped from the hospitality of our entertainers. While on this trip we visited a wonderful cave. A strong current of air swept through the cave with dirge-like sound resembling the music of an Æolian harp. We lighted our torches and entered the subterranean passage. The torches were lighted and we walked through the dust of ages of about five hundred years.

A yawning chasm opened at our feet. Lights

were lowered, steps were hewn in the solid rock now seen winding in a spiral form. We prepared to descend. Turning to the right at the bottom of the stairs the sight that now greeted the vision was resplendent with beauty. The purest stalactites of crystalized carbonate of lime hung from the ceiling. Wreaths of pink colored sulphates of lime, quartz and spar, crystals studding the sides; their beauties made us feel that we were in the fairies' realm.

The melody which had struck our ears at the entrance had subdued and now resembled the distant murmur of a symphony of Mendelssohn executed on some grand organ. This was soon succeeded by unearthly yells, interrupted from time to time by a mocking laugh in a deep bass, such sounds and yells as one might expect to hear in Satan's dominions. Somewhat startled with what we saw and heard, we entered an apartment resplendent with beauty. Stalactites hanging from the roof fully fifty feet from the floor and stalagmites running up to meet them half way, gave the vast chamber the appearance of an alabaster Cathedral with its tiers of columns in regular order, connected by wreaths from column to column.

In the distance we had discovered what we thought was a mass of curious quartz crystals,

THE ENCHANTED CAVE.   95

but on approaching it we saw that it was a living spring jutting from the floor and rising to a height of five feet then parting in the center to fall in a thousand little streams and disappearing forever. As we stood in mute amazement gazing at this beautiful sight a huge animal sprang from his lair and scattered us in every direction. The report of a dozen revolvers vibrated to the unknown depths and some of the fragile formations on the ceiling fell to the floor.

The concussion put out the lights and we groped our way back to the entrance. On our way we found a magnificent mountain lion, eleven feet from tip to tip, the monster which a few moments before had thrown our party into such confusion at the crystal fountain. After an exceedingly fatiguing ascent we again reached the upper air and were satisfied to remain on top of ground for some time afterward."

With good company and well trained steeds our journey passed very pleasantly. We were now approaching the Sierra Nevada Range so called because its sides and tops are covered with perpetual Snow. We dashed along close to the edge of precipices one thousand feet below us and one miss step of our horses would have launched us into eternity in an instant of time. This proximity to danger is very exciting and seemed rather to increase than diminish the pleasure of the ride.

We arrived safely at Carson City on schedule time and I found my good cousin ready to receive me with open arms." What befell Miss Julia in her home in the Sierras must be reserved to another chapter.

CHAPTER XI.

SAUNTERINGS AROUND THE HOLY CITY.

There is no more beautiful place than Salt Lake City. It is in a lovely valley with benches rising on three sides of it and a fertile plain opening away to the south, through which the Jordan winds its silvery way, giving life and beauty in its course. The City is watered by irrigation, the water being brought in ditches, principally, from City Creek. Without this artificial plan of watering the gardens and fields, this valley would forever remain a barren waste; with it, the "The wilderness is made to rejoice and blossom as the rose." Little rivulets are carried along every street and the cotton-wood furnishes ample shade.

Imagine then the City, with singing rills, lovely shade, blooming gardens and sweet-scented orchards of peach, plum, apricot and pear trees, and over all the clear vault of heaven without cloud or mist, and away in the distance the snow-capped mountains whence come the cooling breezes and cause the nights to be refreshing, though the days may be oppressive. This is the most perfect climate on the continent.

The air is perfectly dry, the stars seem brighter and more numerous and the blue vault of heaven seems ten times higher and purer, than in other climes.

Let us take a stroll around the City and get acquainted with it, and the people. Here we are at Temple Block, in the center of the City.

We have come upon a street full of stores. Enormous stocks of merchandise are yearly imported across the plains, and fortunes are rapidly accumulated. On Temple Block, is the Tabernacle and here is where the Grand Temple is to be. When it is finished and consecrated, Jesus Christ is to come again and to take up his abode here and confer degrees on the Saints. Such is their fanatical belief.

To the right of this, is a very pretty house, occupied by the five widows of the late Jedediah M. Grant, one of Brigham's Counselors.

A large barrack looking house, is tenanted by Ezra T. Benson and his four ladies. A mean looking house to the west, by Parley P. Pratt and his nine wives. In that long dirty row of single rooms, half hidden by a beautiful garden and orchard, lives Dr. Richards and his eleven consorts. Wilford Woodruff and five wives reside in another large house still further west. Orson Pratt, the Emerson of Mormonism, and his five wives live near by in a retired country looking house. All these are "Apostles," and their names are inseparable from Mormon History.

Looking towards the north, we espy a whole block covered with houses, barns, orchards and gardens. Here, with his eighteen or twenty families, dwells Heber C. Kimball, First Counselor to Brigham Young, and one of the most sensual, gross and profane men that ever disgraced a community. Strange scenes disturb the seeming serenity of this Mormon Paradise. Passing these, we arrive at the GRAND HAREM, "THE LION HOUSE," in which many of the PROPHET's wives reside.

This is a three-storied building, with peaked gable, and narrow pointed Gothic roof and cost the owner $30.000.

But for the good management of Bro. Brigham, it would have cost more, for when it was ready to shingle, the Prophet had a revelation to the effect that the carpenters should "Shingle the Lion House in the name of the Lord and by the authority of the Holy Priesthood." A large lion carved in stone, is placed upon a pillared portico in front of the edifice, "resting, but watchful," emblematic of Brigham, who is called the "Lion of the Lord."

Passing a row of neat offices we arrive at the Mansion, a large handsome building, excellently built and dazzlingly white. It is balconied from ground to roof; on the top is an observatory, surmounting which, is a bee hive, the Mormon symbol of industry. Eastward still and further back from the street, stands the school-house for the Young family, and further to the right, stands the "White House," occupied by Mrs. Young, the first wife, and her children.

It is a lonesome looking old house, the windows are small and far between; just such a house as you would imagine to be haunted.

To the east, and connected with the Harem by a private passage-way, is Brigham's general business office. This is a large room with three desks on either side; those to the left on entering, being appropriated to the clerks of "Brigham Young, Trustee in Trust for the Church," and those to the right used by the clerks of "B. Young & Co." Still further east and connected by another passage-way, is the private office of the "President." Back of this, is the SANCTUM SANCTORUM; the Prophet's own private bedroom. Here is the "veil," behind which, he receives his "revelations."

He usually occupies this room alone and when he wishes the company of one of his wives, sends a message to that effect. When he is sick he designates one of them to attend upon him, *that* one being usually the reigning favorite.

These with other smaller buildings, make up the improvements on the Prophet's Block, and constitute a small town in themselves.

Struck with the fact that most of the eligible property appears to be in the hands of "the authorities," we continue our walk to Social Hall. This is an adobe building 73x33 feet. In this building is performed dramatic representations from Shakspeare's tragedies to the broadest farces, by a company of Mormon Amateurs. In it too, they "teach the young idea" to dance. The Mormons repudiate waltzes, mazourkas, schottisches, and round dances generally, because they do not want their wives and daughters to be "so intimate with other men."

Cotillions, contra-dances and old fashioned reels are in high esteem, and a Mormon genius has invented a "double cotillion," giving two ladies to each gentleman, a very necessary arrangement as there are about three and one half of the fair sex, to one of the masculine persuasion. The Council House, a two storied building 45 ft. square, next attracts our attention. It is used as a printing office and from it is issued the great Mormon weekly newspaper, the organ of the Church, "The Deseret News." There is an observatory on the top of this building from whence we get a better view of the City than we have heretofore had.

From hence we have the Court House pointed out to us, a large adobe structure, the seat of Mormon law and justice. Here the Territorial Legislature meets to draw the government appropriations, and immediately on its adjournment, the Legislature of the "State of Deseret," meets to make the laws. The United States Government and its officers are entirely ignored by the Mormons, and Brigham Young and his hierarchy have full and exclusive control of everything.

The Arsenal, is a gloomy old pile on the north hill overlooking the City. Here are stored all the fire-arms and ammunition of the "Nauvoo Legion," a military organization formed before leaving the States and of which Daniel H. Wells is Commander-in-chief. This was the formidable army of half clad, half starved ragamuffins that whipped out our army under Johnson, sent by Buchanan to conquer the Mormons in 1857, which expedition cost our government twenty millions of dollars.

Another notable building is the Tithing office, a large spacious building, with cellars, storerooms and offices attached. Each person on entering the Mormon Church, is required to pay the tenth of his or her property to the Lord's servants for "building up temples, or otherwise beautifying and adorning Zion, as they may be directed from on high." Having tithed their property, they must tithe their yearly income for the same purpose, thus rendering about one fifth of their substance to the Church.

The ladies give a tenth of their fowls, a tenth of the eggs, and then a tenth part of the chickens hatched, without regard to loss. Everything sent as tithing, must be of the very best, as the Lord will accept nothing that has a blemish or imperfection. But the Prophet was not satisfied and so had a law passed making it legal for the people to transfer their property to the Church. He then commanded them to consecrate their all to the Church, on pain of everlasting hell.

This was at the time of the Reformation when the doctrine of blood-atonement was freely preached.

Jedediah M. Grant, one of Brigham's Counselors said in a sermon:

"Brethren and sisters, we want you to repent and forsake your sins. And you who have committed sins that cannot be forgiven through baptism, *let your blood be shed, and let the smoke ascend,* that the incense thereof may come up before God as an atonement for your sins, and that the sinners in Zion may be afraid."

So great was the excitement caused by this doctrine, that many came and offered up their lives on the altar of sacrifice. This altar was erected within Temple Block by this same bloody Priest, J. M. Grant.

Those who did not feel like being killed, appeased the anger of the Almighty by deeding and consecrating their property to the Church, for Brigham was shrewd enough to see that if their substance was in his power, he could hold the rod over them and they would be powerless. Said Brigham, in speaking of this law, "Men love riches, and can't leave without means. Now if you tie up the calf, the cow will stay."

Here we are at Temple Block, but we have described this elsewhere and will say in passing, that on this block is the Tabernacle, and north of this, a frame-work covered with boughs and called the "Bowery." This is used for conference meetings, being capable of accommodating 8.000

THE TEMPLE. 105

persons. It is a singular scene when filled with well-dressed and earnest devotees, who listen with rapt attention to utterances of their spiritual leaders and take it all in as gospel truth.

In the north-west corner of this block is the Endowment house, where the secret ordinances of Mormonism are administered. For a more complete description of the sink of iniquity, see chapter on Mormon Mysteries.

On the eastern side of this square, are the foundations for the famous Temple. They are of solid rock, and have already cost over a million, in material and labor, more than the whole of the Nauvoo Temple when complete. It is extremely doubtful whether this building will ever be finished, and many think it was never the intention of Brigham that it should be finished, because he knew that he could not carry out his promises made to the people, that Jesus Christ would re-appear when the Temple was completed and Himself administer the endowments to his chosen people.

We have now visited the greater part of the public buildings and have seen Salt Lake City as it appeared on a beautiful October day, in the year of our Lord, 1862.

CHAPTER XII.

HAPPENINGS IN SALT LAKE CITY.
From Mrs. Burlingame's Journal.

We are now in the midst of a polygamous community. The Mormon polygamist has no HOME. Some have their wives in small disconnected houses. Some have long low houses and on taking a new wife, add a room to the row. Some have but one house and crowd them all together, without regard to comfort, or even decency. When they live in different houses, the husband has to give each wife her turn to cook for him and he honors their tables with his presence in rotation. Jealousies the most bitter, reproaches the most galling and acrimony without end are the consequences of the slightest partiality.

It is impossible for any man to equally love several women at the same time. The nature most in unison with his own, will most attract him. To feel partiality and not exhibit it, is unnatural, to exhibit it and have it pass unnoticed by a jealous woman is impossible. Any husband might feel to kiss his wife gladly; to go round a table and kiss half a dozen is no joke. Every word, every look, every action has to be weighed, or else there is bitterness, and vituperation. Warmth of feeling, tenderness of attachment, is called by the worst of Mormon epithets "Gentilish." " Man must value his wife no more than anything else he has committed to him, and be ready to give her up at any time the Lord calls on him," Said Brigham one Sunday afternoon; and J. M. Grant followed the remark by saying, " If God, through his prophet, wants to give my women to any other man more worthy than I am, there they are on the altar of sacrifice; he can have them and do what he pleases with them." In spite of the constant effort to keep the women quiet they are discontented and unhappy.

The first wives are the most miserable. In one of Brigham Young's sermons he said,—

Now for my proposition; it is more particularly for my sisters. Men say, My wife, though a most excellent woman has not seen a happy day since I took my second wife.' 'No, not a happy day for a year,' says one; and another has not seen a happy day for five years. It is said that women are tied down and abused; that many are wading through a perfect flood of tears.

I wish my own women to understand that what I am going to say is for them as well as others, and I want those who are here to tell their sisters, yes all the women of this community. I am going to give you from this time to the 6th day of October next, for reflection, that you may determine whether you wish to stay with your husbands or not, and then I am going to set every woman at liberty and say to them, "Now go your way, my women with the rest; go your way."

And my wives have got to do one of two things, either round up their shoulders to endure the afflictions of this world, and live their religion, or they may leave, for I will not have them about me. I will go into heaven alone, rather than have scratching and fighting around me. I will set all at liberty. 'What, first wife, too?'

Yes, I will liberate you all. I know what my women will say; they will say, 'You can have as many wives as you please, Brigham?' But I want to go somewhere and do something to get rid of the whiners."

We were invited to spend the day with Brother Shurtleff a regular old patriarch with five wives and twenty children. When dinner was ready we were seated in the places of honor to the right of the host and the first wife took her place opposite her husband. The plural wives with their children were seated in their order the grown up sons and daughters of the first wife near their mother. There were twenty-one persons at the table including Mr. Burlingame and myself. The patriach in a very feeling manner called down blessings on us and all mankind and but for the knowledge that we were in a polygamic household we would have enjoyed our visit immensely.

After dinner the youngest wife and favorite combed and brushed the patriarch's flowing white locks and seemed as fond of him as any new made bride. We chatted with the different wives, praised their children, walked around the farm and inspected the garden, orchard, cattle and grain, and truly the Lord had blessed this modern Abraham in his basket and in his store.

When we were ready to depart Bro. Shurtleff loaded us down with apples, pears and peaches and with kind adieus to the five Mrs. Shurtleff, and a hearty hand shake from Bro. S. we stepped into our carriage and drove back to the City.

In October, 1862, great excitement prevailed because the government was sending troops to Utah. The Mormons looked upon this as a menace and feared that another "war" was imminent. They declared that the soldiers should never cross the Jordan, but in spite of their threats, on a bright morning in October, Col. Connor, with his command marched into and through Salt Lake City and established his camp on the "bench" about three miles east of the City, and overlooking it.

The people were made to believe that the new Governor and Judges had something to do with the coming of the troops and decided hostility was manifested towards them. Gov. Harding's message to the Legislature commented very severely on polygamy and aroused a great deal of feeling. Then a bill was sent on to Congress to enable the Federal officers to carry out the laws and to punish polygamy. This was the last straw that broke the camel's back and a great indignation meeting was held in the Tabernacle. The Governor and Judges were denounced and threatened and a committee appointed to invite them to leave the Territory. Threats of personal violence were freely used and the situation was becoming anything but agreeable. We were all sitting quietly one evening in the parlor of the Governor's house, when we were startled by loud cries and oaths outside, and in a moment more, missiles and rotten eggs were being thrown in rapid succession against the house.

Windows were broken and glass flew in every direction; they were mobbing the Governor's house. He let them alone until they got tired; he said that he could stand it if Brigham could for the owner would have to repair the damages.

After this we kept our house well guarded. We had two six shooters, and Mr. Burlingame insisted on my learning how to use one of them, one double barrelled shot gun, one axe, one club and several other weapons, offensive and defensive. The Mormons would loudly threaten to hang Mr. Burlingame as they passed the house, but we soon became accustomed to their style and paid no attention to it. Mr. B. went where he pleased, day and night, but kept his eyes open and his revolvers ready. We were warned and watched and surrounded by spies who were listening for every word, to report to Brother Brigham.

Notwithstanding these unpleasant surroundings, we all like Salt Lake and greatly enjoy our residence here. We have ascertained to our satisfaction that the Mormons are cowards and when they find we are not afraid of them they will let us alone. The Cavalry at Camp Douglas had a review a few days ago and came down pretty near the City, and the people came running to us frightened half to death thinking they were going to be attacked. The Mormon leaders have forbidden their wives and daughters to come and see us so we have to seek our society at Camp Douglas.

CHAPTER XIII.

LIFE AT CAMP DOUGLAS.

From Mrs. Burlingame's Journal.

There are no more gay and hospitable people, than the Military. About fifteen of the officers stationed at Camp Douglas had brought their families. Houses were built, and though rude, were made very home-like, and comfortable. Gen. Connor's residence was quite aristocratic and pretentions. Surgeon Reid and lady, were also housed very comfortably. Capt. McLean and Madam, entertained handsomely. Capt. Hoyt and his lovely wife were good and kind. Mrs. Reid, an accomplished lady born in the Bermuda Islands, of English parents, (her father was Governor General of the Islands,) was as kind to me and mine, as if she had been my sister. She had brought on her carriage and horses from California and scarcely a week passed that we did not go out prospecting, or visiting some place of interest in the neighborhood of the City.

One fine morning, we were off to visit Great Salt Lake. We passed Hot Springs where the water would boil an egg, and crossed the sandy plain on a gradual descent to the Lake which is surrounded by long stretches of baked and cracked soil, over which is an incrustation of dazzling salt crystals. The water of Salt Lake, is the strongest natural brine in the world, holding in solution, over 22 per. cent. of different salts. Its dark, sluggish waves forcibly remind the gazer, of the Dead Sea, and were it not that this is 4.200 feet ABOVE, and that 1.000 feet BELOW the level of the Ocean; THIS locked in by surrounding mountains, while THAT rolls over the "cities of the plain," it would be easy to fancy one self away in Palestine and looking on that scene of human corruption, decay and desolation.

After partaking of a sumptuous lunch, several of the party, attempted to take a swim in the Lake. We could neither sink nor swim and were pretty much in the condition of the man who put on cork shoes when going in to bathe.

Some of us were so unwise as to have our

SWIMMING IN SALT LAKE. 115

mouths open and the surf dashed the salt water into them, and so strangled us, that we did not recover our equilibrium for some time. We decided that swimming in Salt Lake was not a success, and on coming out, we found ourselves in the condition of Lot's wife to all outward appearances. Mrs. Reid said that the next time she went to Salt Lake, she should keep on the outside of it, and not get it on the outside of her.

Before starting for home, we visited a cave near by, said to have been the rendezvous and grave of a band of Indian warriors. They were fleeing from their victorious enemies, when they espied this cave and, unfortunately, sought it for safety. The victors guarded its entrance carefully, allowing none to escape. All died from starvation and their bones lie bleaching in this desert cave. The sensations produced by this dreadful sight, cast a damper over the remainder of our visit.

As winter approaches, everything assumes an air of gayety about the Camp. Preparations are on foot for a New Year's Ball. We are all looking forward to the event, with much pleasure. Last week, one fine morning, Mrs. Capt. McLean sent down horses "all saddled and bridled," and requested our presence at breakfast. We hastily prepared ourselves and mounting our steeds, rode up to the Camp. Breakfast not being ready, several of the party proposed a ride up the Canon as an appetizer.

We started in gay spirits up Emigration Creek and the ride was truly delightful. The birds were singing sweetly in the tree-tops of cottonwood, pine and hemlock, the water of the Creek dashed over little precipices and dancing joyously in the sunlight, fell from height to height, making many picturesque little falls. The air was cool and delicious, and so pure that we felt as much exhilarated by it as if we had been taking laughing gas. Our horses also felt it and were difficult to manage. After a glorious ride, we returned to a breakfast fit for a king and we did it ample justice.

We are here 4.200 feet above the level of the Ocean. From the tops, of these mountains, we had marine shells brought to us, showing conclusively, that at some period of time, Old Ocean rolled over the tops of these mountains. Truly this is a land of wonders!

New Year's Eve came at last and with it, the grand ball. The Hall was draped with evergreens, and the stars and stripes floated over all, assuring us that we were under the protection of the freest government on earth,

What a contrast between this assembly and the Mormon anniversary that we attended last summer! The Military officers with their wives, the Federal officers and their families, and the Gentile residents of Salt Lake City made up the company. Not a man but would have drawn his sword in defense of his wife or sweet-heart, not a man but would have scorned a polygamist, and would have resented any attention from one, to his wife. These were the brave and noble sons of California who were ready at any and all times to go to the front and do battle for the Union, but who were kept here to see that the Mormons did not inflate the minds of the Indians and cause an outbreak while the Union was in danger.

The ball was opened by a grand quadrille, in which Governor Harding, General Connor, Judges Burlingame and Drave participated. After this, the dancing was confined principally to the younger members of the company. The *menu* was elegant and costly, and the festivities continued into the wee sma' hours. We remained until the next morning and after breakfast, witnessed a most beautiful sight from the top of the Camp Observatory, viz: the valley of the Great Salt Lake in the distance, and the Oquirrh Range beyond. The sun shone down upon the whole and lighted up the mountain peaks with molten gold, while the snow-capped mountains sparkled like diamonds as the sun dissolved the rays of light into all the colors of the rainbow. We returned to our home in the City, thankful that we were under the protecting care of the noble officers and men of Camp Douglas.

Everything that they can do, is done to make our stay here, pleasant and profitable.

Gen. Connor has been very kind to the poor among the Mormons, often sending them flour and provisions. The Apostates would have been cut off "root and branch," if the troops had not been here. The Morrisites were starved, burned out, beaten and murdered before the army came in, but now, the Mormons dare not touch them. They will not employ them to do any kind of work and consequently, they have no way of living; Brigham through the law of consecration having possessed himself of most of their property.

The troops are in the City a great deal, going back and forth as much as they please, much against the wishes of the leaders. They are creating great dissatisfaction among the rank and file of the Mormons, and though Brigham has given strict command that his people shall not trade with the soldiers, they are constantly doing it, on the sly. I have bought flour of my Mormon neighbors at $11 per hundred, and sold it to the Camp for $15, the said neighbors, not daring to sell it direct for fear their Prophet would find it out. Brigham is now my bitter enemy and says he would rather have forty "Gentile" men among his people, than one "Gentile" woman. I like my life here, very much. There is just enough of danger to make it exciting and just enough of adventure to make it interesting.

CHAPTER XIV.

PRACTICAL POLYGAMY.

From Mrs. Burlingame's Journal.

Yesterday I disguised myself by dressing like a Mormon "sister," with a slat sun bonnet and a calico skirt and sacque, and started out in search of a house. The emigrants had just come in and it was a common thing for them to go house hunting. I had heard that there was an old English couple who had a young woman, the man's second (plural) wife, chained in a dark damp cellar.

They wanted to rent a part of their house, so I went in. They eyed me very closely, but I was so familiar with Mormon slang and so fluent in talking their religion that like a certain other party that we read of, I deceived the very elect.

They showed me the house above stairs but with all my hints about the cellar I could not induce them to take me down there. While rumaging around the kitchen I hear a young child cry. Looking at the old lady I as much as said, 'that cannot be yours.' She understood me and she carelessly remarked, "it is my husband's by his second wife." "Where is it" I said. "O, down there," pointing to the cellar way; "let her behave herself next time." My suspicions were fully confirmed when I heard a weak voice call out, "I am so faint, can't I have a cup of tea?" "No" growled the old woman "you dont deserve it."

I could get but little out of the old woman, except that the woman had been refractory and was there to be punished. I went out burning with anger, but suppressing it as much as possible. I called into a neighbor's house and there learned the dreadful truth. This old pair of ghouls had come over from England some two years ago bringing with them one of the many foolish young girls that are inveigled into Mormonism by the hellish arts of Mormon "Elders." After being in Utah a few months she was made acquainted with celestial law and told that she must be sealed to the old man. She rebelled and called in her brother to aid her. He went to Brigham about it but he said it was only a whim and she would soon get over it.

Accordingly she was taken to the Endowment House and there sealed to the old man. After this they were very cruel to her and treated her worse than a plantation slave. She was made to do all the work in the house and also work in the field. She was starved and beaten and abused in all the brutal ways that a brutal man can invent. When her baby was but three days old this fiend in human shape renewed his abuse and when the poor, feeble, suffering creature protested, he dragged her from her bed by the hair of her head, and threw her down into the damp cellar on a little heap of straw. As soon as she could muster strength she climbed up the stairs and then he CHAINED HER IN THE CELLAR. This neighbor took her food and drink and put it through the grated window to her. It is needless to add that she is insane from cruelty and want and that Brigham has sent for her brother to come and take her down South. He fears the "Gentiles" will get hold of it, so my Mormon "sister" says. I came home with a heavy heart resolved to do something to help them poor women if possible.

On my way home I stepped in to a millinery store to look at some bonnets. The lady in charge asked me if I had come in with the last emigration. I told her I had. "Has your husband taken a second wife yet." I told her he had not. "Well" said she "he will have to do it, and you had better pick out one that will suit you and get him to take her." "Oh, it is hard" said she, "very hard; but no matter, we must bear it, for it is a correct principle and there is no salvation without it. We had one, [meaning a plural wife,] but it was so hard both for my husband and myself that we gave her up at the end of seven months. She had been a good servant, but as soon as she became a wife, she became insolent, and told me she had as good a right to the house and things as I had and 'you know,' she said "that didn't suit very well.

"But," continued she, "I wish we had kept her and I had borne everything, for we have got to have one, and dont you think it would be pleasanter to have one you had known; than a stranger?" I told her I thought it would be if it had to be done, but I hoped my husband would not take one. She said, "He'll have to do it, if you and he want to be saved."

Another case illustrating the PROXY doctrine as it is called came to my knowledge a few days ago. A Mr. Cushion was engaged to be married to a Miss Susan McBride, when he was taken sick and died. He had been a great favorite of Bro. Heber C. Kimball who was very desirous that he should be exalted and glorified in the Celestial Kingdom. This could not be done unless he had a family.

The Mormon doctrine is that unless a man has a wife or wives and children he will have to attach himself to some other man's family and become a servant. Single men and women are absolutely worthless either in this world or the next except as ministering angels to some God or Goddess in the future world. So, as Heber was determined that Brother Cushion should be somebody in the Celestial Kingdom, he insisted that Miss McBride should marry the man she loved, BY PROXY, portraying to her in vivid colors how she could glorify and exalt him by so doing and telling her that she was bound by her promise to do so.

The poor girl, puzzled and troubled, and desirous of securing as much glory for the man she loved as possible and of being his for all eternity, consented. Heber now had to cast about to find some "saint" who would thus sacrifice himself for his dead brother. Robert T. Burton, Sheriff of Salt Lake County, and Collector of Internal Revenue for the United States Government was the man selected. He was ready to undertake the task, for as he said, "He was willing to do any thing to please Brother Kimball."

The poor girl was sealed to Cushion for eternity and married to Burton, as his third wife, for time. Thus disposed of, she was taken home and domiciled with the two Mrs. Burton. These worthy matrons were not pleased with the appearance of a new wife and, claiming their rights as the only real wives, who had been sealed to their husband both for time and eternity, resolved at once to make it exceedingly uncomfortable for the new comer. This they did effectually, and Susan's life was wretched beyond expression. But time passed and she became the mother of several children, all of whom, of course, belonged to Bro. Cushion.

Susan was not allowed to associate or eat with the family. She had but one small room in which she cooked, ate, slept and spun, [all Mormon women are expected to make cloth for themselves and children at least,] while the other two had splendid chambers and parlors, for Burton is wealthy. When she complained to Burton, he said,—"Susan, you know I have only married you for time, and you must not expect the same privileges I grant to my other wives, who are married for eternity, and who will glorify me in the celestial kingdom. You ought to be thankful for what you do receive, and not fret about my other wives."

The first wife takes full control of Susan's children, in contradiction of this complex and unnatural relationship, and the mother is frequently obliged to see them severely punished and suffer in silence. One day, the first wife's boys and one of Susan's were in the barn, doing some mischief. The first wife went out and commanded the boys to come away. Her own boys ran by, unharmed, but when Susan's boy, the youngest of the lot, came out, she caught him, beat him, threw him on the ground and kicked him.

Heber C. Kimball is the man that usually sees to all these matrimonial matters and decides when it is time for a man to take more wives. One day he met Mr. Taussig a Prussian brother. "Brother Taussig," said he, "are you doing well?" "Yes, sir," was the reply. Then you must do well for the church too, said the second President: "How many women have you?" "Two, Sir." "That is not enough, you must take a couple more. I'll send them to you. Do you hear." "Yes, sir," said Bro. T. On the following evening, when he returned home he found two women sitting there.

His first wife said: "Brother Taussig, [all the

women call their husbands, "brother,"] "these are Sisters Pratt." They were two widows of Parley P. Pratt. A son of P. P. P. was about to marry Heber C. Kimball's daughter and wanted the house these women lived in. *Hinc illæ lacrimæ.* One of the ladies, Sarah, then said: "Brother Taussig, Brother Kimball told us to call on you, and you know what for." "Yes ladies," replied Brother Taussig, "but it is a very hard task for me to marry two." The other remarked, "Brother Kimball told us you were doing a very good business and could support more women." Sarah then took up the conversation: "Well, Brother Taussig, I want to get married, anyhow."

The good brother replied, "Well, ladies, I will see what I can do; and let you know." The next day, Brother Taussig visited the Bishop and effected a compromise. By marrying Sarah he was released from the other.

After a while, Sarah became dissatisfied and applied to Bro. Brigham for a divorce. Bro. Taussig was summoned before the President, who alone can grant a divorce. Brigham says that the tom-foolery of the people in getting divorces keeps him in pin money. Brother Taussig made but feeble resistance to the suit of the gentle Sarah and the divorce was granted, and the clerk called for the $10. For not having the money Bro T. received a good cursing and Sarah was retained in the royal presence, with the assurance that it was "no divorce" until the money was brought in. Bro T. went into the street, borrowed it, and brought it into the office,—and thus ended this disgusting serio-comic conjugal farce.

Similar stories and experiences came to me almost every day as my business led me to go much among the people. In my rounds I saw young girls of fifteen married to old men of eighty. In one house-hold a mother and two daughters were wives to one man. As I entered this home, the two young women were tending their babies while their mother was doing the work about the house. There seemed to be a good deal of comfort and even happiness in this house-hold, as curious as it may seem

The mother would be more interested in the family and less likely to be jealous of her daughters. One of our nearest neighbors, a Mr. Sharkey is married to three sisters and they get on tolerably. The older sister is no longer treated as a wife but must content herself with assisting her more fortunate sisters. A man by the name of G. D. Watt is married to his half sister and this case has been often cited as the worst phase of polygamy. Watt brought his half sister to Salt Lake City; took her to Brigham, and wished to be married to her, for his second wife. Brigham objected, but Watt urged that Abraham took his half sister and "reckoned he had just as good a right as Abraham." The point was knotty and difficult.

If Abraham's example justified polygamy, then it must equally justify this action. "God blessed Abraham although he did it, and ought to bless me if I do it." The girl happened to be good looking and Brigham, to cut the gordian knot he could not untie, married her himself. After a few weeks, Brigham had a "revelation," and sending for Bro. Watt, told him that he (Watt) was right after all and that it was just as lawful in him as in Abraham, and accordingly, G. D. accepted his half sister to wife, from the arms of Bro. Brigham.

It is a constant source of surprise to see how these women can be made to assent to and practice such a horrid system, but when we remember that they are taught to think that God has re-established a priest-hood on this earth; that this priest-hood is almost immaculate and quite infallible, as a priesthood, we can understand how they can blindly believe and blindly obey all they are commanded. Not only is the prospect of securing their own salvation, but also that of their children held out to those misguided women.

The Mormons believe that the pure seed of the house of Jacob cannot be lost. They are "children of the covenant made to Abraham." They also believe that the children of those who have been "sealed up to eternal life," can never be lost. The woman is told that if she marries a young man and he apostatizes, both she and her children will share in his ruin and be forever lost. To marry an old, well-proven, and sealed man, will secure her own salvation and that of her children, and if she does not enjoy all the temporal happiness she might with a young man, she will enjoy more of the spirit of God and receive eternal exaltation in the Celestial Kingdom. Then, too, these men can save their dead relatives, who have never heard the gospel, i. e. Mormonism.

The dead can hear the gospel in spirit, and their friends in Zion can receive the ordinances by "proxy." The inducements to marry an old Saint rather than a young one are, salvation for themselves, their children yet unborn, and their dead kindred. With the devotion of eastern idolaters, they immolate themselves on the shrine of their faith, and who shall question the purity of their motives, or the sincerity of their hearts? It may be asked "why do they not fly when they awaken to their error and find that they have been duped and grossly deceived." Fanaticism may be strong, but self-love is stronger. Many would fly, but they are mothers, and they would have to desert their children.

The mother's love often overcomes the woman's shame. These women can be respected in Utah, but not out of it. Most of them are poor and could not leave if they would. If they should attempt to leave with "Gentiles," the Mormons would follow them and their own lives and also the lives of their protectors would have to pay the penalty. Many a Gentile in these mountain regions and also many a Mormon saint lie in the brush or mountain canyons with a pistol ball through their skulls, for daring to interfere in Mormon domestic arrangements. How can we blame these poor women who are thus enslaved and chained as it were, to the rock of polygamy. Bound by nature, that is, the love of their children, bound by custom, that is, the opinion of society, bound by their religion, that is, the fear of everlasting destruction if they disobey the priest-hood, they are in the clutches of inexorable fate.

CHAPTER XV.

A PROSPECTING EXPEDITION.
From Mrs. Burlingame's Journal.

One day last week a man came to see Mr. Burlingame, and when I told him he had gone up to Montana with Governor Doty, he seemed a good deal disappointed. I said if there is anything you would like to say, I will tell Mr. B. when he returns and he will do anything he can for you. He hesitated a long time and then he said, "1 have something of importance to communicate before I leave the Territory.

Judge Burlingame has been very kind to my people, (the Morrisites) and I feel like doing something for him. Brigham has swindled me out of twenty thousand dollars and I mean to get even with him. He has sworn that the "Gentiles" shall not find the gold and I want to show him that he can't prevent it."

I was by this time, thoroughly interested, and as he was going away in a few days, I asked him to tell me where the mines were. After a little delay, he took a paper and pencil, made a diagram and explained the route and told me if I would get some reliable parties to go, he would meet us at Big Cotton Wood Creek, about seven miles from the City. Mrs. Reid and I had prospected several Canyons and as Gen. Connor had left word for us to have men and conveyances whenever we called for them, I sent word for her to be at my house, at six o'clock sharp, on Thursday morning, with provisions for three days and two of the best California miners in Camp.

Accordingly just as I was sipping my coffee, and the hand was on the hour and minute, she drove up with an outfit for prospecting, of the most approved kind. We rode through Salt Lake City, much in the style of the middle ages, with outriders and retainers and all the appliances for camp life.

When we arrived at Big Cotton Wood Creek, we looked around but no Mr. W. was to be seen. I had feared as much for I knew how much these people dread Brigham's vengeance. Here was a dilemma indeed, so I got out my map and told Mrs. Reid and Mrs. McLean that I felt sure we could find the place and that I was willing to go ahead if they were. They consented and on we went. It was a very hot day, and we were crossing a sandy plain, devoid of water, for twenty miles. Our mules began, toward-noon, to show signs of giving out, and to make matters worse, our escort had taken another road, thinking that we were going to Little Cottonwood, where we had been a few days ago.

Mules will lie down and refuse to rise when very thirsty, and we looked every moment to see ours do so. Every traveler carries a keg of water on these plains, so we gave ours to our mules, and coaxed them along as best we could. Presently, and when we least expected it, they began to prick up their ears and to go faster. The driver said, "We are all right now, they smell water. We must be near the Canyon." And sure enough we soon spied the mouth of Bingham Canyon and saw the Creek fringed with green, with grateful eyes.

Our escort just then rode up, and together we entered the Canyon and made our camp. The old man that was to show us the mines, was out hunting his oxen and did not return until late at night. Meanwhile, Mrs. McLean, who was a first rate cook, prepared our dinner and the prospectors took their pans and went to work. They had not been gone long, when they returned and reported that they had found "pay dirt," and had washed up several pans and got "the color." This greatly elated our party and visions of wealth floated before our wakeful eyes all night as we fought musquitoes and bed-bugs in the cabin of the old Jack Mormon.

Some of us became so disgusted that we made us a bed in an old covered wagon which stood in the yard. Morning came however, and with it, the problem of how to get the old man to show us the mines. Mrs. Reid offered him considerable money, and a share in the mines, and told him he should be protected by the military. He said he should risk his life by going with us, "But" said he, "I don't care much about living anyway, so I'll go with you."

We got into the ambulance, bright and early, and started up the mountain. After riding four or five miles the way became too difficult for our mules even, and we proceeded on foot. The rocks gave evidence of rich mineral deposits on every side. We would look up at almost perpendicular walls and exclaim, "The gold and silver are here in quantities, why can we not find it?"

We finally arrived at a ledge of copper and silver ore mixed, the copper largely predominating. This will some day be worked for its copper alone. Further up we found another ledge composed of lead and silver which contained a large per cent of silver. We gathered up all we could carry and went back in gay spirits to our ambulance. On having our ores assayed at Camp Douglas, they were found to be very rich, and the General immediately made ready to locate claims.

Two companies were formed; "The Vedette Copper and Silver Mining Co." and "The Bingham Canyon Silver Mining Co."

Thus were discovered to the "Gentiles," the first mines in Utah; and according to present appearances, there are no better mineral deposits in these mountains than "The Bingham Canyon Mines."

CHAPTER XVI.

MORMON MYSTERIES.

As marriage is a religious ceremony more than a civil institution, the Mormons insist on having it performed by an ecclesiastical dignitary. Civil marriages are mere contracts sanctioned by law, but dissoluble at the option of the contracting parties. They believe that unless married, the saved will not enjoy any "glory" in the next world; and if not married on earth, cannot be married afterward, therefore they "MARRY FOR ETERNITY."

These marriages are always performed in their sacred and secret Temple, in a singular manner, and are called "Sealings."

The Mormons constantly inveigh against the licentiousness of the "Gentiles," and extol polygamy as the cure for this and all kindred evils, but, in fact, these sealing ordinances are only a cloak to cover the grossest licentiousness. A woman comes to Salt Lake who cares little or nothing for her husband. Some of the "Heads" take a fancy to her and want to marry her. The position of the husband is such that it would be impossible to get a divorce, so she is sealed to her paramour and still remains with her husband, the Mormons claiming all the children by her first husband, to belong to the sealed one in the Celestial Kingdom. Hence, no man is certain of his dearest wife's virtue, or his warmest friend's honor. Suspicion and jealousy, are the inevitable result. It is very common for a woman to be married to one man for time and sealed to another for eternity.

They also believe in salvation for their dead relatives. Hundreds of devout and fanatically sincere people are immersed in behalf of their dead relatives, males for men, and females for women. But their salvation must be consummated in the same manner as that of the living. "They will be nowhere," says Kimball, "unless they have wives;" and these immersed people are therefore MARRIED for their dead. And as the glory of the dead, as well as the living, depends on the size of their families, these accommodating "proxies", ALSO RAISE CHILDREN FOR THEIR DEAD.

That these practices should be indulged in, under the sanction of religion, is infamous. It is a bitter satire on human purity and progress, a disgusting and palpable proof of human depravity.

Much has been said of the Mormon Endowment, and oaths are administered obliging the persons taking them to undergo a violent and cruel death if they reveal the "Mystery."

The following drama will give a very correct idea of this unique and significant allegory.

THE ENDOWMENT.

Dramatis Personæ.

ELOHEIM, or *Head God*, Brigham Young.
JEHOVAH, Heber C. Kimball.
JESUS, Daniel H. Wells.
MICHAEL, *or Adam*, W. C. Staines.
SATAN, W. W. Phelps.
APOSTLE PETER, Orson Pratt.
APOSTLE JAMES, John Taylor.
APOSTLE JOHN, Erastus Snow.
WASHER, Dr. Sprague.
CLERK, David O. Calder.
EVE, Miss Eliza R. Snow.
TIMOTHY BROADBRIM, *a Quaker*, Wilford Woodruff.
DEACON SMITH, *a Methodist*, Orson Hyde.

PARSON PEABODY, *a Presbyterian*, Franklin D. Richards.
ELDER SMOOTH-TONGUE, *a Baptist*, Phineas S. Young.
FATHER BONIFACE, *a Catholic*, George A. Smith.
BROTHER and SISTER JONES,
BROTHER and SISTER WHITE,
SISTER MARY BROWN, *to be sealed*
  to BROTHER WHITE,
Several other candidates.

ACT 1. SCENE 1.

[*Enter Candidates.*

CLERK. Good-morning, brethren and sisters. Be seated. Brother White, please state the time and place of your birth, date of your marriage, and the time when you were baptized into the church.

BRO. W. I was born November 3d, 1801, in the town of Portsmouth, in New Hampshire. I was married January 1st, 1824, and was baptised into the church April 1st, 1860.

CLERK. Have you paid your tithing punctually? If so, produce your receipts. [These are read, and handed back.] That is sufficient. You are entitled to receive your endowments.

Sister White, will you state when and where you were born, and when you became a member of the church?

SISTER W. I was born September 18th, 1815, in the State of New York, and became a member of the church in 1852.

WASHING AND ANOINTING.

CLERK. Sister Mary Brown, please state when and where you were born, and when you became a member of the church.

SISTER MARY. I was born June 20th, 1849, in Great Salt Lake City, and was baptized into the church in 1860.

[The Clerk propounds the same questions to all the candidates, and enters their answers in the record.]

CLERK. You will now proceed to the washing-room, the brethren on the right, and the sisters on the left.

APOSTLE PETER. You will remove your shoes, that the dust of earth may not pollute the holy ground on which you are about to tread.

[The candidates are then washed in tepid water, and each member blessed with a blessing peculiar to each. They are then pronounced clean from the blood of this generation, and a new name is given to each by the Apostle Peter. They then return to the waiting-room, where the brethren are anointed with oil, the sisters receiving their anointing in their own washing-room.

This ceremony consists of pouring olive-oil upon the head of each, well rubbed into the hair, nose, eyes and mouth, and allowed to run down over the person. It is accompanied by a blessing, similar to that received at the washing. Brain to be strong, ears to be quick to hear the words of God's servants, eyes to be sharp to perceive, and feet to be swift to run in the ways of righteousness. This is the anointing administered preparatory to being ordained a "King and Priest unto God and the Lamb."

Thus greased and blessed, the "garments" are put on. A dress of muslin or linen is worn next to the skin, reaching from the neck to the ankles and wrists, and in shape like a little child's sleeping garment. Over this a shirt, then a robe, made of fine linen, crossing and gathered up in plaits on one shoulder, reaching to the ground before and behind, and tied around the waist. Over this is fastened a small, square apron, similar in size and shape to a masonic apron, made of white linen or silk, with imitation of fig leaves painted or worked upon it. A cap made from a square yard of linen, and gathered into a band to fit the head, and white linen or cotton shoes, complete the dress of the candidates.]

SCENE 11. CREATION.

ELOHEIM SEATED UPON HIS THRONE.

[*Enter* JEHOVAH, JESUS, and MICHAEL.

ELOHEIM. "Ye powers of Heaven!" This day hath Satan, our rebellious foe, been vanquished.

THE EARTH CREATED. 143

Lest he again presumptuous rise, let us create new worlds, and people them with beings who by slow degrees shall rise and fill the place of those by him deceived. Go forth, ye heavenly messengers; examine well the boundless realms of space, and bring report from thence back to the Eternal Throne.

JEHOVAH, JESUS, AND MICHAEL, [all]. Eternal Father! Great Eloheim, Maker and King of the celestial worlds. Joyful we go, thy mandates to fulfil.

[*Exeunt* JEHOVAH, JESUS, and MICHAEL.

ELOHEIM. Far into chaos proudly ride my messengers. Winds bear them onward, o'er the deep profound.

[*Re-enter* JEHOVAH, JESUS, and MICHAEL.

JEHOVAH, JESUS, AND MICHAEL, [all]. Almighty Ruler. The way is clear. Send forth thy Word alone, and worlds will rise, and circle into space, obedient to thy call.

ELO. "Silence, ye troubled waves! your discord end. Thus far extend, thus far thy bounds. This be thy circumference, O world!"

JEH. Behold the Earth. "Matter unformed and void; darkness profound covers the abyss."

MICH. But see, "the Spirit of God outspread, and vital virtue infused, and vital warmth throughout the fluid mass. Like things to like!

The rest to several place disparted." And in the air, "the Earth, self-balanced, on her center hangs."

Elo. "Let there be light."

Jesus. "Hail! Holy light. Offspring of Heaven, first born."

Elo. The light is good. Let darkness flee into the shades of night, and light make up the day.

Mich. Hark! "the celestial choirs, when orient light, exhaling first from darkness, they behold,—birthday of Heaven and Earth; with joy and shout, the hollow, universal orb they fill."

Elo. "Let there be a firmament amid the waters, and let it divide the waters from the waters."

Jeh. "Behold the firmament,—expanse of liquid, pure, transparent, elemental air, diffused in circuit to the uttermost convex; partition firm and sure, the waters underneath from those above dividing."

Jesus. The water still doth compass all the Earth, moulding all the plastic mass, and doth implant, within her genial breast, the seeds of various life.

Elo. "Be gathered, now, ye waters under Heaven, into one place and let dry land appear." Land, free from your prison-house, arise, and be called Earth. Ye waters,—seas. Now, "let the Earth put forth the verdant grass, herb yielding seed, and fruit-tree yielding fruit after her kind, whose seed is in herself, upon the Earth."

Mich. Oh, sight sublime! The Earth, till now, barren and fruitless was; "her universal face" now clothed in "pleasant green." Listen, ye Gods! The morning stars, which in the vast expanse of Heaven, circle their rounds, together sing. The sons of God, swift-winged angels, shout for joy.

Elo. "Let there be lights, high in the expanse of Heaven, to divide the day from the night; and let them be for signs, for seasons and for days, and circling years; and let them be for lights, as I ordain their office, in the firmament of Heaven, to give light on the Earth." Two great lights,—great for their use to man,—the greater to have rule by day, the less by night; the stars I also set in the high firmament, to illuminate the Earth, and rule the day in their vicissitude, and rule the night, and light from darkness to divide."

Jeh. Behold, "the thousand, thousand stars, that now appear, spangling the hemisphere," the luminaries bright, that rise and set, and crown the glory of the fourth new day.

Elo. "Let the waters generate reptile, with

spawn abundant; living soul; and let fowl fly above the Earth, with wings displayed, on the open firmament of Heaven, and the great whales, and each soul living, each that creeps, and in the waters generate, and each bird of its kind,—let each be blessed;" "be fruitful, multiply, and in the seas and lakes, and running streams, the waters fill: and let the fowl be multiplied."

Jesus. Let Heaven rejoice, let Earth be glad, and hail the dawning of the fifth new day.

Elo. This is the sixth and last morn of creation. Let every creature forth, from his genial mother, cattle and creeping thing, and beast of earth, each of his kind. All, all is good, and pleasing in my sight.

Jesus. "Now Heaven in all her glory shines. Earth, in her rich attire, consummate, lovely, smiles; air, water, earth, fowl, fish and beast are here, and yet there wants the master work of all yet done; a creature endued with reason, which erect may stand, and self-acknowledged, govern all the rest."

Elo. "Let us make man, in our own image, man in our similitude, and let them rule over the fish and fowl of sea and air, beast of the field, and over all the earth, and every creeping thing, that creeps the ground." Thou art created male and female, in the form and likeness of the Gods. Go forth, be blessed; "be fruitful, multiply, and fill the earth, subdue it, and throughout dominion hold" over all, all else that breathes upon its bosom. Now all is finished, all complete and perfect. Immortal Gods, let us to our high seat ascend, that from our lofty throne our perfect works we may behold.

[To represent the creation of man, Jehovah, Jesus, and Michael stroke each candidate separately, pretending to form; and by blowing into their faces, pretend to vivify them. They are then supposed to be as Adam, newly made, and perfectly ductile in the hands of their makers. A deep sleep then falls upon the new Adam, and ribs are extracted, out of which, in another apartment, their wives are formed. They are then commanded to awake, and their wives are introduced to them; after which they file by twos into the garden.

The four sides of this room are painted in imitation of trees, flowers, birds, wild beasts, etc. The ceiling is painted blue, dotted over with golden stars. In the center of it is the sun, a little further on the moon, and all around are the stars. In each corner is a Masonic emblem. In one corner is a compass, in another the square, the remaining two are the level and the plumb. On the east side of the room, next the door is a painted apple tree, and in the northeast part of the room, is a small wooden altar.]

SCENE 111. Garden of Eden.

[*Enter* Adam and Eve, and Endowees.

Eve. "Well may we labor, still to dress this garden,—still to tend plant, herb and flower, our pleasant task enjoined." "Let us divide our labors," each where seemeth good; and thus, as night draws on, our task will be accomplished.

Adam. "Sole Eve, associate sole, to me beyond compare, above all living creatures dear! A doubt possesses me, lest harm befall thee, severed from me; for thou knowest what hath been warned us, what malicious foe envies our happiness."

Eve. "Offspring of Heaven, and all Earth's Lord! That such an enemy we have, who seeks our ruin, both by thee informed, and from the parting angel overhead; but that thou shouldst my firmness therefore doubt, to God or thee, because we have a foe may tempt it, I expected not to hear."

Adam. "Daughter of God and man, immortal Eve,—for such thou art; from sin and blame entire; I, from the influence of thy looks, receive access in every virtue. 'Why shouldst not thou like sense within thee feel when I am present, and thy trial choose with me,—best witness of thy virtue tried."

Eve. "If this be our condition, thus to dwell in narrow circuit, straitened by a foe, how are we happy still, in fear of harm?"

Adam. "O woman, best are all things as the will of God ordains them; therefore go; for thy stay, not free, absents thee more."

Eve. "With thy permission then, and thus forewarned," I go.

[Enter Satan, in the form of a serpent, half-man, half snake. He discovers Eve in a bower of roses, and watches her at a distance.]

Satan. "Thoughts, whither have ye led me?—what hither brought us? Hate, not love, but all pleasure to destroy." [He approaches Eve.] "Wonder not, sovran mistress, fairest resemblance of thy Maker fair, at my appearance, half man, half beast, but approach and view this goodly tree, the fruit of which such wonders work."

. Eve. "Serpent, we might have spared our coming hither," for "of this tree we may not taste or touch; thus hath our God commanded."

Satan. Indeed! Hath God then said, that of the fruit of all these garden trees ye shall not eat, yet lords declared of all in earth or air?

Eve. "Of the fruit of each tree in the garden we may eat, but of the fruit of this fair tree, amidst the garden, God hath said, 'Ye shall not eat thereof, nor shall ye touch it, lest ye die.'"

Satan. "O sacred, wise, and wisdom-giving plant; mother of science! Now I feel thy power within me clear, not only to discern things in their causes, but to trace the ways of highest agents, deemed however wise. Queen of this universe! Do not believe these rigid threats of death;—ye shall not die. Your tyrant ruler knows full well, that in the day ye eat thereof, ye shall be as Gods, and good from evil know. "Goddess humane, reach then, and freely taste."

[Satan plucks the fruit and presents it. Eve receives it, and after considerable hesitation, tastes, and finally eats it. Adam soon after enters.]

Eve. "Hast thou not wondered at my stay? Thee have I missed;" for I have tasted of the tree to us forbidden, and such delight till now have never felt. Taste thou, [offers him the fruit,] and be a God.

[Adam stands amazed and sorrowful, dropping a garland from his hand.]

Adam. "O fairest of Creation! Some cursed fraud of enemy hath beguiled thee, and me with thee hath ruined; for with thee certain my resolution is to die." [He eats.] Oh, fruit delicious, fit indeed for Gods. From us withheld, lest being Gods, we cease to obey our tyrant Lord.

[They soon begin to see their true condition. They reproach each other. They discover their nakedness, make aprons of fig-leaves, and wear them. The voice of Eloheim is heard in another part of the garden.]

Elo. "Adam, where art thou? Why hast thou fled and hid thyself? What hast thou done?"

Adam! O Lord, my Maker and Preserver! Thy voice I heard, when thou didst walk amid the trees, but being naked, I did fear to see thy face. Confusion dire and shame filled all my soul.

Elo. "Who told thee thou wast naked? Hast thou then eaten of that tree, to thee forbidden?"

Adam. The woman whom thou gavest me did give this fruit unto my lips; and I did eat.

Elo. O woman, fair but frail. Why hast thou done this deed of sin?

Eve. "The serpent me beguiled, and I did eat."

[The serpent, abashed retires to a secluded place.]

Elo. Come forth thou monster of iniquity, and receive thy just reward.

SATAN. [aside] "Now let the mountains on me fall, rather than brave His dire displeasure."

ELO. "Because thou hast done this, thou art accursed above all cattle, each beast of the field. Upon thy belly grovelling thou shalt go, and dust thou shalt eat, all the days of thy life. Between thee and the woman I will put enmity, and between thine and her seed: her seed shall bruise thy head, thou bruise his heel." And thou, O Eve, thy sorrow I will greatly multiply by thy conception: children thou shalt bring in sorrow forth, and to thy husband's will thine shall submit; he over thee shall rule." And thou, O Adam, "because thou hast hearkened to the voice of thy wife, and eaten of the tree concerning which I charged thee, saying, 'Thou shalt not eat thereof;' cursed is the ground for thy sake; thou in sorrow shalt eat thereof all the days of thy life; thorns also and thistles it shalt bring thee forth unbid; and thou shalt eat the herb of the field; in the sweat of thy face shalt thou eat bread, till thou return unto the ground; for thou out of the ground wast taken; know thy birth; for dust thou art, and shalt to dust return."

ELO. [To Jehovah, Jesus, and Michael.] "Behold the man is now become as one of us, knowing good from evil; and now, lest he in some unguarded hour put forth his hand, take of the tree of life, and live forever, we must forth from hence expel him." We will place from Eden eastward cherubims, and flaming sword, turning which way soever he may attempt an entrance.

ADAM. "O miserable of happy! Is this the end of this new, glorious world?—and me, so late the glory of that glory? Accursed of blessed, hide me from the face of God, whom to behold was once my height of happiness."

EVE. "O unexpected stroke, worse than of death! Must I thus leave thee, Paradise?—thus leave thee native soil,—these happy walks and shades, fit haunt of Gods, where I had hoped to spend, quiet though sad, the respite of that day that must be mortal to us both? O flowers! that never will in other climate grow, my earliest visitation and my last at even, which I bred up with tender hand; from the first opening bud, and gave ye names! Who now shall rear ye to the sun, or rank your tribes, and water from the ambrosial fount? Thee, lastly, nuptial bower! by me adorned with what to sight or smell was sweet! From thee, how shall I part, and whither wander down into a world, to this obscure and wild? How shall we breathe in other air, less pure, accustomed to immortal fruits?"

ELO. O man, thy cries of penitence and woe

have reached my ears. I will a plan unfold, obedience to which, rendered with deep humility, shall by degrees redeem and bring you back to Heaven.

My holy priesthood I henceforth establish upon Earth. To those endowed with that high calling, as unto me, shalt thou in reverence bow. Their power supreme, commands indisputable, in my stead, I appoint them unto you. They are to act henceforth, as I myself.

[Here oaths of inviolable secrecy, with the penalty of throat-cutting, are administered to the awe-stricken and intimidated neophytes. They are sworn to render implicit obedience to the priesthood, and to depend upon them for everything; especially not to touch any woman unless given through the priesthood.

A sign, a grip, and a key-word are given to the endowees, and the FIRST DEGREE OF THE AARONIC PRIESTHOOD is conferred.]

ELO. You are now endowed with one law of purity, one key of truth, and one power of priesthood. Go forth into the world, ye fallen ones, and seek for truth. Obey the voice of God and his holy priesthood, and I will send to Earth a Savior, that through faith and obedience you shall again inherit your lost estate, and again enjoy the ambrosial fruits in the celestial kingdom of God.

[*Exeunt all.*

SCENE 1V. THE WORLD.

]*Enter* ADAM, EVE, Endowees, and Sectarians.

TIMOTHY BROADBRIM. I feel the movement of the Spirit to speak unto thee. Thou knowest that the world is lost in sin and wickedness. But ye should "resist not evil," but "overcome evil with good." "If a man take away thy cloak, give him thy coat also." Raise not thy hand to harm a fellow-creature. "Charity suffereth long and is kind!" See that no brother be in want; look ye after the widow and the fatherless.

DEACON SMITH. Brethren and Sisters,—I rise to address you a few words, founded upon the following passage of Scripture:—"And there shall be weeping and wailing, and gnashing of teeth." Oh, this is a fearful doom. Oh, ye sinners, hear. There is a lake which burns with fire and brimstone; you are on the very brink; do you not see thousands of the damned weltering in its burning waves? You are, as it were, on a greased plank, sliding, and sliding, as swift as the wheels of time can roll, down to this awful gulf. [Sisters begin to shriek and faint.] Flee from the wrath to come.; fly to Jesus; come to the mourners' bench; cry mightily to God for help. He alone can save you. Come,

come, come to Jesus. Brethren and sisters, sing,—

"Where shall the guilty soul find rest?" etc.

Parson Peabody [speaking through his nose.] My dear hearers, this is a fallen world. We are all in the gall of bitterness, and in the bond of iniquity. Satan, the great enemy of mankind, is ever seeking our destruction. Let us close our hearts against his wiles, and come to Jesus, and if we are of the elect, foreordained from before the creation of the world, we shall be saved; and if not, we shall be lost. We can do nothing of ourselves. We are in the hands of a just and wise God, who doeth all things well.

In the language of the divine poet,—

"If you can, if you can't;
If you will, if you won't;
You'll be damned if you do,
You'll be damned if you don't."

Let the brethren remember their covenants, and let them bring their offspring to the altar, and there consecrate them to God, through the ordinance of sprinkling; and if they are to be saved, they will be saved. Otherwise, though not a span long, they will go down to the bottomless pit.

Elder Longface. Brethren,—The subject of my discourse will be found in the following text: "Whom he did predestinate," &c.

We learn from this,—1st, That we are sinners. 2d, We need a Saviour. 3d, That we must be baptized by immersion. 4th, That we should exclude from the communion-table all such as are not immersed. 5th, That many are called, but few chosen. 6th, That those who are chosen will be saved, without their own action in the matter. 7th, That those who are not chosen will be damned, no matter what they do, in and of their own strength; and lastly, in order to have the least opportunity to be saved, you must join the Baptist Church.

The Lord grant that many may embrace the truth as it is in Christ Jesus, and unite with "our church," and be saved. The brethren will sing,—

"O, when shall we see Jesus," &c.,

FATHER BONIFACE [with pages, robes, candles, &c.]. *Te Deum laudamus.* [They sing.] O Divine Queen of the skies, Holy Mother of God, to Thee we lift up our voices. Grant us Thy divine intercession with Thy dear Son, that we, through His precious blood, may be made clean. Bless Thy believing children, make them faithful to their Holy Father the Pope, diligent in counting their beads, and saying their matins and vespers. O Holy Mother, keep them from all sin; especially grant them grace to eat no meat on Friday, and we will ever adore and bless Thee, Father, Son, and Holy Spirit. Amen.

Let the choir sing *Ave Maria. Benedicite.*

[*Enter* SATAN.

SATAN. Good-morning, brethren. I love you all; you are my friends. I am gratified to find you so faithful in assisting me to build up my kingdom. Rest assured you shall be rewarded. You shall be kings and princes when I succeed in setting up my throne upon the Earth.

Enter Apostles PETER JAMES and JOHN.

PETER. Why dost thou tempt the children of men, and lie in wait to deceive them?

SATAN. "Let me alone. What have I to do with thee," thou follower of Jesus? I know thou hast the holy priesthood of God,—

PETER, JAMES, AND JOHN, [all.] And in the name of the Lord Jesus Christ, and of the holy priesthood, we command you to depart from hence.

[The Devil foams, hisses, and rushes out, chased by the Apostle Peter.]

JAMES. My children, hearken now unto my voice. When in these last days God saw the lost condition of mankind, his heart was moved with pity, and He sent with me Peter and John, and commanded us, saying, "Go ye to Earth, and seek me a good man of the lineage of Joseph, who was carried away into Egypt, and of the lineage of the prophets, even Joseph Smith." Restore to him the lost priesthood. Bestow upon him the keys of power; make him Prophet, Seer, and Revelator, and let him re-establish my church upon the Earth." Behold, this was done, and the same power and authority has now descended from Joseph to Brigham. Hear ye him, the representative of God on Earth. Him reverence and obey, and ye shall advance toward the kingdom of Heaven.

[An oath, penalty. the heart to be plucked out, with agonizing details, is administered. The utmost secrecy is impressed, and the SECOND DEGREE OF THE AARONIC PRIESTHOOD is conferred, with signs, grips, &c.]

ACT 11. SCENE 1.

[*Enter Apostles* PETER, JAMES, and JOHN, with the candidates for endowment.

PETER. Dearly beloved, you are now in the way of salvation. Be faithful to each other, and all your brethren. Betray not the secret things of Zion to the ungodly gentiles. Think not with your own thoughts, but come to the priesthood. They are the mediators between God and man. Obey, without murmuring, whatever they command, though it may seem to you unjust or unreasonable. Your hearts are not so fully sanctified as to enable you to judge as to the merit of their acts. Be ever ready and willing to forsake father or mother, husband or wife, houses or lands, for the glory of Zion, and the upbuilding of God's kingdom on the Earth. And more especially, brethren, as you value your eternal salvation and temporal welfare, speak no evil of the Lord's anointed.

[An oath is now administered, with particulars the most disgusting and revolting. Another sign, key-word, and grip, are communicated, and the FIRST DEGREE OF THE MELCHISEDEC PRIESTHOOD is conferred.]

SCENE 11.

ANOTHER ROOM WITH AN ALTAR IN THE CENTER; ON IT THE BIBLE, BOOK OF MORMON, AND BOOK OF DOCTRINE AND COVENANTS. JEHOVAH IN THE ROOM AND ELOHEIM IN THE NEXT, LOOKING ON. THE CANDIDATES ARE RANGED ROUND THE ALTAR. THE APOSTLES ARE ALSO PRESENT.

PETER. You are now in a saved condition, and acceptable in the sight of God. You are to enter on the work of the Lord, in truth and sincerity.

"Behold now," saith the Lord, "the wicked and ungodly gentiles; they have slain the Prophet Joseph, persecuted the saints, and mocked at my priesthood. Therefore, O Israel, arise in thy strength, go forth and revenge the wrongs of my people on this perverse generation. They have spilled the blood of the saints, and wasted their substance. Therefore let their blood be spilled, and let their substance be wasted."

Let the curse of God rest on this nation and Government. Let wars and famine, and cruel pestilence overtake them, and let the Church of God, in its glory and power, rule over all the nations, and fill the whole earth.

Therefore, brethren, be ye vigilant; and let no opportunity pass to vindicate the name of your God; and if you cannot do it, teach it to your children. Let them take it from their mother's breast. Teach it to them from your bed of death, and leave it for an inheritance, that all people may know that the God of Israel has set His hand to gather His people, and to destroy the wicked from off the face of the earth.

[Here another oath is administered, binding the endowee to revenge the death of Joseph Smith on this generation; to cherish constant enmity toward the United States Government, doing all in his power for its overthrow; to baffle its designs, to refuse submission aud renounce all allegiance. and to obey the church authorities, and no other.

Curses the most frightful, penalties the most barbarous. accompany the obligation. to add to its binding efficacy. and to insure secrecy. A new sign, grip, &c., complete the SECOND DEGREE OF THE MELCHISEDEC PRIESTHOOD.]

JOHN. You are the children of the Most High, endued with powers and blessings. Your robes of righteousness, which you must henceforth wear, in token of your covenants, are on the wrong shoulder, and none but God's priesthood can set them right. [The robes are changed to the other shoulder, and the candidates are stationed in a circle, around the altar.]

PETER. Little children, you are now the chosen of God to carry on His mighty work, and He, through His servant, will teach you how to pray, that your supplications may reach the eternal throne, and call down an immediate answer.

[Peter kneels on his right knee, takes hold of the hand of one of the standing brethren, all of whom are united by a fantastic intertwining of hands, and prays slowly, all repeating his words after him:]

"O, God, ruler of the celestial world, we have this day taken upon ourselves covenants and powers from thy hand. Make us faithful to those covenants; and if we obey not thy commands, let thy curses descend upon our heads.

Make us faithful in Zion and in the upbuilding of her cause, and at last receive us into thy celestial kingdom, with all the gifts, powers, and blessings this day pronounced upon the faithful in Israel. Amen.

PETER. Brethren, you are now members of the holy orders of God's priesthood. Henceforth you are entitled to all the blessings and privileges of the same.

[The endowees, fitted for Heaven and celestial glory pass "behind the vail," a new name is whispered very softly and quickly to each; certain marks, resembling the Masonic square and compass, are cut in the under garment, on the left breast; also a similar one on the knee. The candidates are then ushered into the full light and glory of the celestial kingdom. The brethren turn back to the vail, and admit their wives, whose garments are marked in a similar manner.]

SCENE 111. THE CELESTIAL KINGDOM.

IN THE CENTER OF THIS APARTMENT IS AN ALTAR, NICELY CUSHIONED, WITH A CUSHIONED LEDGE TO KNEEL UPON. THE MEN KNEEL UPON ONE SIDE AND THE WOMEN UPON THE OTHER, EACH BROTHER HOLDING THE HAND OF HIS WIFE, ALSO OF THE WOMAN TO WHOM HE IS TO BE SEALED, WITH THE PATRIARCHAL GRIP. THE CEREMONY OF SEALING

FOR ETERNITY THEN COMMENCES.

Eloheim. Children of Earth, you have been redeemed by the blood of the Lamb, and by the power of my holy priesthood. You have been faithful unto the end, and shall now receive a crown of glory.

Brother and Sister White and Sister Brown, arise and receive your blessings. Brother White, as I gave Eve unto your father Adam, while he was yet pure and holy, so give I your wife unto you to be yours to all eternity.

Now Sister White, as Sarah the mother of the faithful gave Hagar unto Abraham, I command you to give unto your husband another wife, that he may be exalted in my Celestial Kingdom. (The wife stands on the left of her husband, while the bride elect stands on HER left.)

Elo. Sister White, are you willing to give this woman to your husband, to be his lawful and wedded wife, for time and eternity? If you are, you will manifest it by placing her right hand within the right hand of your husband.

(The right hands of the bridegroom and bride being thus joined, the wife takes her husband by the left arm as in the attitude of walking.) Eloheim continues,—"Do you, Brother White, take Sister Brown by the right hand, to receive her unto yourself, to be your lawful and wedded wife, and you to be her lawful and wedded husband, for time and for all eternity, with a covenant and promise on your part, that you will fulfill all the laws, rites and ordinances pertaining to this holy matrimony, in the new and everlasting covenant, doing this in the presence of God, angels, and these witnesses, of your own free will and choice?

Bro. White. "Yes."

Elo. Do you Sister Brown, take Bro. White by the right hand and give yourself to him to be his lawful and wedded wife, for time and all eternity, with a covenant and promise, on your part, that you will fulfill all the laws, rites, and ordinances pertaining to this holy matrimony, in the new and everlasting covenant,—doing this in the presence of God, angels, and these witnesses, of your own free will and choice?

Sister Brown. "Yes."

Elo. In the name of the Lord Jesus Christ, and by the authority of the Holy Priesthood, I pronounce you legally and lawfully, husband and wife, for time and all eternity; and I seal upon you the blessings of the holy resurrection, with power to come forth in the first resurrection, clothed with glory, immortality, and eternal lives; and I seal upon you the blessings of thrones and dominions, and principalities, and powers, and exaltations; together with the blessings of Abraham, Isaac and Jacob; and I say unto you, be ye fruitful and multiply, and replenish the earth, that you may have joy and rejoicing in your posterity, in the day of the Lord Jesus.

All these blessings, together with all other blessings pertaining to the new and everlasting covenant, I seal upon your heads, and enjoin faithfulness unto the end, by the authority of the Holy Priesthood, in the name of the Father, and of the Son, and of the Holy Ghost. Amen."

The candidates dress, get a lunch, and return to the "celestial kingdom" to hear a lecture by Kimball, explanatory of the whole scheme. The signs, tokens, marks, and ideas are many of them taken from the Masonic Order. "The intention of the mystery is to teach unlimited obedience to the church and treason against the country."

CHAPTER XVII.

HISTORY OF WOMAN.

Woman is looked upon and treated by all heathen nations as an inferior being, created for the convenience and comfort of man.

According to the ancient Rabbis, the rib which had been taken from Adam, was laid down for a moment, and in that moment a monkey came and stole it, and ran off with it, full speed. An angel pursued, and though not in league with the monkey, he could have been no good angel; for, overtaking him, he caught him by the tail brought it maliciously back, instead of the rib, and out of the tail was woman made. What became of the rib with which the monkey got clear off 'was never to mortal known.'

The Hungarians think it infamous to be governed by a woman,—and when the crown fell to a female, they called her King Mary instead of Queen.

Aristotle calls woman a monster, and Plato makes it a question whether she ought not to be ranked among the irrational creatures.

Mahomet, too, was not the only person who has supposed that women have no souls. Among the Afghans, twelve young women were given as compensation for the slaughter of one man. Six for cutting off a hand, an ear, or a nose; three for breaking a tooth, and one for a wound of the scalp. By the laws of the Venetians, and certain other Oriental people, the testimony of two women was equivalent to that of one man.

According to the Brahmins, the widow who burns herself with the body of her husband, will, in her next state, be born a male; but the widow who refuses to make the self-sacrifice, will never be anything better than a woman, let her be born as often as she may.

The Jew begins his public prayer with a thanksgiving to his Maker for not having made him a woman. The Moors do not allow women to enter their mosques or places of worship.

Mussulmen hold that there is a separate paradise for women, considering them unworthy to occupy the same as the men, except such beautiful women as are assigned to the male occupants as a reward for a virtuous and religious life on earth. "Sit not in the midst of women," said the son of Sirach, in his wisdom; "for from garments cometh a moth, and from women, wickedness."

"It is a bad thing," said Augustine, "to look upon a woman, a worse to speak to her, and to touch her, worst of all." John Bunyan thanked God that he had made him shy of the women. "The common salutation of women I abhor," said he, "their company alone, I cannot away with." "Look at the very name· woman," says another author, "it evidently means woe to man, because by woman was woe brought into the world."

The Turk does not exclude woman from his heaven, but she is there only to minister to his passions and wants. She bears to his lips the golden goblet, filled with the nectar of the gods.

The Indian hunter believes his squaw, as well as his faithful dog, will bear him company to those shadowy hunting-grounds beyond the dark river.

Among all these heathen and degraded nations, polygamy has prevailed. Among them all, woman has been but the slave of the stronger sex. Her feelings have been outraged, her spirit crushed, her heart broken; or, which is still worse, her nature has become imbruted and insensible to all the finer feelings and nobler impulses of her sex.

Foremost in the ranks of her oppressors stood Brigham Young. Following in the footsteps of Mohammed, he declared that women have no souls,—that they are not responsible beings, that they cannot save themselves, nor be saved, except through man's intervention. To be saved, a woman must be sealed to a good man, —he can save her; or, if he does not, her sins will be upon his head. Under this system, woman was created expressly for the glory of man; hence the more women and children a man has, the more glory.

This doctrine is openly put forth in the most disgusting form.

Said Brigham, in a public discourse, Sept. 20th, 1856,—

"It is the duty of every righteous man and woman, to prepare tabernacles for all the spirits they can; hence if my women leave, I will go and search up others who will abide the celestial law, and let all I now have go where they please."

It may seem very strange, that so many women are led into the snare of polygamy. The most specious arguments are advanced, and inducements held out, by the wicked and designing leaders of the Mormon Church, to blind and deceive unsuspecting and simple-minded women. They are told that "the laws of Christendom differ widely from those of the other three fourths of the whole family of man;" that they are the laws and practices of "a wicked and perverse generation," and differ also from the doctrines taught in the Bible. It is a noticeable fact that the Bible is only quoted on the subject of polygamy. On all other topics, the books of Mormonism are used. These being, as already shown, adverse to their favorite institution, resort is had to the Old Testament Scriptures.

Abraham is constantly cited as the great exemplar and pattern. It is urged that the family order observed by him is the order established among celestial beings, in the celestial world. That God sanctioned the practice, and is himself a polygamist.

One of the most important innovations upon the established doctrines of the church, is in relation to the Godhead. In April, 1852, Brigham put forth the startling doctrine that Adam is God, and to be recognized and honored as such! This announcement created some consternation among the Mormon theologians, and some of them had the courage to oppose it. The following is the Revelator's own exposition of this doctrine:—

"When the Virgin Mary conceived the child Jesus, the Father had begotten him in his own likeness. He was not begotten by the Holy Ghost. And who is the Father? *He is the first of the human family;* and when he took a tabernacle, it was begotten by his Father in heaven, after the same manner as the tabernacles of Cain, Abel, and the rest of the sons and daughters of Adam and Eve. . . .

It is true that the earth was organized by three distinct characters, namely: Eloheim, Yahovah, and Michael, [Adam;] these three forming a quorum, as in all heavenly bodies, and in organized element perfectly represented in the Deity, as Father, Son, and Holy Ghost.

"When our Father Adam came into the garden of Eden, he came with a celestial body, and brought *Eve, one of his wives*, with him. He helped to make and organize this world. He is Michael, the Archangel, the Ancient of Days. *He is our Father and our God, and the only God with whom we have to do.* . . . Jesus, our elder brother, was begotten in the flesh by the same character that was in the garden of Eden, and who is our Father in Heaven."

Mahomet is the great exemplar and prototype whom Brigham Young aimed to imitate, and doubtless he took from the Koran his ideas about the deity of Adam. Thus in chapter two of the Koran, we have the following:—

"And when we said unto the angels, 'worship Adam,' they all worshiped him, except Eblis, [Lucifer,] who refused."

That many virtuous and high-minded women should infinitely prefer to unite their fortunes to ONE good man, rather than to have each a wicked husband who could bring her no exaltation in another world. "Shall such virtuous and innocent females, though they may be poor, and low in the scale of fortune's partial smiles,—shall they be denied to choose the objects of their love? Must they, through the operation of hideously contracted laws, be virtually doomed to resort to infamous prostitution, entailing disease, infamy, and death upon themselves and their offspring, or to marry an inferior grade of corrupt, and vicious men,—debauchees, gluttons, drunkards, and idlers,—or remain in perpetual celibacy, and frustrate the designs of their creation, and violate the first and foremost command of God,—to multiply and replenish the earth?"

They are pointed to Jacob, also, who had several wives, and who was the father of the twelve patriarchs, after whom all the tribes of Israel were named. From one of these wives, Christ himself lineally descended. Various other instances are cited from the Jewish Scriptures,—especially the fact that the Lord gave unto David some of the wives of Saul. "Hereby we learn that God himself gives many wives to those who are faithful, AND TAKES THEM AWAY FROM TRANSGRESSORS." The faith of Abraham was indorsed by Christ and his Apostles, and those who have the same faith are called heirs of the promise. Hence an effort is made to bring the

New Testament also to the support of polygamy notwithstanding it is so plainly condemned in that volume. Indeed, it is unblushingly asserted that not only the Apostles, but Christ himself practiced polygamy! "The grand reason," said J. M. Grant, one of the First Presidency, in a discourse delivered in the Tabernacle in Great Salt Lake City, "why the gentiles and philosophers of that school persecuted Jesus Christ, was because he had so many wives. There were Elizabeth and Mary, and a host of others, who followed him."

To Abraham and Sarah was the promise made—"In thee and thy seed, shall all the nations of the earth be blessed." The sisters are called upon to follow the example of Sarah, and to give plural wives to their husbands, even as Sarah gave Hagar unto Abraham. "If you suffer with her [Sarah] you shall reign with her. You shall be heirs of the same promise, and crowned with glory in the celestial world."

By these specious arguments and falsehoods, are thousands lured on to destruction.

CHAPTER XVIII.

A SISTER'S REVELATION.

From Mrs. Burlingame's Journal.

Yesterday I received a long visit from a Mormon sister. She had seemed to want to confide in me several times before and as we sat conversing rather confidentially, the subject of polygamy came up. I said, "How is it that so many women of intelligence and refinement, come to Utah and are to be found in polygamy, either as first, or plural wives?" Said she, "I will tell you. When the Elders teach this doctrine at all to their new converts in other countries, they never teach it to unbelievers, they lay great stress upon the assertion "that in no case would any man be allowed to take a second or third wife without the entire consent and approval of the first. This statement, though false and deceptive, naturally silences the fears of many women, by leading them to believe that their husbands could never enter polygamy without their consent and approval.

The theory is that when a Mormon wishes to take another wife, Brigham Young must have a revelation that the Lord desires the brother to extend his kingdom, and directs the patriarch to obtain the consent of the first wife to take another. Then he must get the consent of the parents or guardians of the bride elect, he must make love to the damsel herself, showing her that in his devotion to God and for the upbuilding of His kingdom on Earth and in the Heavens, he desires to take her for a second wife that he may save her soul and make her a queen in the Celestial Kingdom. In this he is presumed to obtain the acquiescence of the damsel herself. This is the theory. Should the "Lord" disapprove, the suit is ended.

A sister once resisted the attempt of her husband to take another wife and in her agony exclaimed, "Surely the Lord will not sanction this thing which will break my heart." A friend in

high station laid his hand upon her arm and
pointed to the residence of Brother Brigham
and emphatically remarked, "Your Lord resides
up there." "Ah my friend," she said, "It is too
true that Brigham Young is the only God with
whom we have to do. His will is law, his hatred, death." I said, why do not the women resist this dreadful law. She smiled sadly, shook
her head and with a shudder continued. "One
poor wife tried that plan and her fate was too
terrible to relate." My curiosity was greatly
excited and I urged her to tell me the story.

"You know" she began, "that the Revelation
says that if any man have a wife who holds the
keys of this POWER, and he teaches her the law
of my priesthood, as pertaining to these things,
then SHE SHALL BELIEVE, and administer unto him
or she SHALL BE DESTROYED, saith the Lord your
God, for I WILL DESTROY HER." Well, the husband of my friend saw a lovely girl and was determined to have her. He consulted his wife
but she was bitterly opposed and to make matters worse, my friend was the daughter of one
high in the priesthood. She went to her father
and besought his protection, but without avail.
He told her she must obey the Celestial Law.

For many days and nights she moaned and
wept. She refused to eat or drink. Her pite-

ous appeals to her husband and father, were enough to melt a heart of stone. At length, wearied and worn, she gave her consent and proceeded to the Endowment House to perform the "sealing." With a dazed and wandering mind but a calm exterior, my poor friend went through the ceremony until the last and crowning act, and when she took the hand of the "bride elect," and placed it in the hand of her husband, she gave a shriek which pierced the very heavens and sank lifeless to the floor. When she revived, reason had fled and the bride and groom carried to their home a raving maniac."

"Oh, my poor friend, once so bright, so lovely and so happy." And tears flowed freely down her face as she continued, "I could take you to see her any day if I dared." She is now gentle and quiet unless she sees the second wife when she calls to mind everything that happened that dreadful day. She has one little room about ten feet square and here she spends most of her time, sometimes wandering aimlessly through the garden and grounds of her home, now hers no longer. I said, "This must be an exceptional case is it not?" She replied, "You would be perfectly astonished if you knew how many insane women there are in the territory, particularly, first wives."

They are not often allowed so much freedom as my friend, but are kept in under-ground and out of the way places, and when it can be done safely, they are "disposed of" in such a way as to give their husbands the least trouble, in other words, the Revelation is obeyed to the letter and they are destroyed."

My anger was by this time fully roused and I said, "I would never submit, I would fly to the desert before I would yield to such degradation." "Alas, my friend," said she, "that too, has been tried, but with nothing but disastrous results. I had a friend some years ago who tried to escape and her bones lie bleaching on the sands of the desert. She was a well educated, energetic little woman and had a son and daughter born in England. She had loved and respected her husband very much and he had promised her that if she would come to "Zion" he would never go into polygamy. He was a good man and fully intended and desired to keep his word. One day President Young sent for him and counseled him to take a second wife, and when he plead his promise to his wife, the angry prophet said "I command you in the name of Israel's God, that ye do this thing, or judgment will be laid to the line and righteousness to the plummet and you shall be sheared down."

This threat could not be disregarded by either husband or wife and the second wife was brought home. With her entrance at the front door, peace, happiness and hope fled away, and the poor wife endured in silence as long as human nature could endure. Children came, and then the husband began to be cold and distant toward her. This broke her heart and she resolved to get away. One evening we were strolling about Emigration Square, and we stopped to talk with some of the emigrants. We learned that several families, not liking the appearance of things, had resolved to go on to California and were intending to join a party of Gentile emigrants at a distance of about one hundred miles west of Salt Lake City. My friend resolved to go on with them. She gathered a few household goods as rapidly as possible and in the dead of night, conveyed them to the camp of the emigrants. Next morning, before day, they started. Nothing occurred during the first day to disturb them and they hoped that they were to be allowed to go away peaceably.

Towards night of the second day, as they were traveling along in a narrow canyon, they were startled by the yells of Indians, as they supposed. About a dozen men armed to the teeth and disguised as Indians fell upon these defenceless people and murdered them in cold blood. The children were brought back to Salt Lake City as well as all the property of the emigrants. These children remembered the horrible scene and told it to those who had them in charge."

"This is too outrageous to endure," I said. "Why do not the Mormon women rise EN MASSE and make an appeal to Congress to take up their defense?"

"Oh," she replied, "although many Mormon women pine and die under polygamy, they are, as a rule, too firm in the faith to appeal to their enemies, as they call the "Gentiles." They would suffer death itself if necessary, for their religion, and while they groan under polygamy, they believe in it."

This seemed very strange and absurd to me, and I asked her to explain it. She began by saying, "You know we are all taught to believe that God has established his priesthood again upon earth, through Joseph Smith and that we are led as the children of Israel of old, by direct divine revelation. We are taught that there are a plurality of Gods and a plurality of worlds, and that each of these worlds has a God to rule over it. Joseph has a world which will be peopled by his descendants and over which he will reign as God. His wives will be Goddesses, and will each rule her own descendants under Joseph as head God. The same is true of Bro. Brigham, Bro. Heber and others in the order and according to divine right.

We are instructed that if a wife loves her husband truly and unselfishly, that she will want to exalt him to be the God of a world, and she can only do this by giving him many wives and thus increase his family and help to people his Earth. In withholding wives from her husband, a woman is selfishly and wickedly preventing him from being a God, and being exalted in the "Celestial Kingdom." "Is it possible" I asked, "that all Mormon women hold these views?" "Oh, not all now, because many are here who have altogether renounced in their own minds, the whole system, but do not dare to avow their sentiments. These are kept in subjection by threats of destruction in case of disobedience.

When a wife is weak in the faith, she is visited by the proselyting sisters who go about meddling in other people's affairs, preaching submission to the poor heart-broken wives, and making love-matches. They remind the wives, that woman was cursed in the Garden of Eden, and that we must take up the cross, for no cross no crown and when the wife is broken in and tamed, the husband rejoices and the "sisters" join in prayer and relate all the blessings awaiting those who live in obedience to the "Celestial Law." This generally lasts until the first wife gets a glimpse of the second wife, or hears of her husband taking her to the theater, or the dance and then "the devil," is raised again and the whole performance must be repeated."

"There ought to be a stop put to these terrible proceedings and I think our government ought to be ashamed to let such outrages be perpetrated upon citizens whether they petition or not." "There are a good many difficulties in the way of doing anything in that way," said she. "That has been tried a number of times, but you see the "Secret Orders," take care of that matter.

"There are the Grand Archees of the Gods, The Danites, The Order of Enoch and the Traveling Brethren, and the resident brethren. Then we have our representative in Congress and our newspapers that are bought up in the interest of the Church. A large amount of money is kept in bank in Eastern cities to use whenever it is thought necessary to prevent any unfriendly legislation. Then the Indians, who are nearly all Mormons, are ready to tear up the telegraph lines, attack the emigrants and Gentile settlers, whenever the Mormon Bishops give them the order. So you see that there is but little chance to do anything to successfully resist the power of the Church. You know several times quite large numbers have apostatized and they have always been "cut off" and persecuted until they were glad to get away with their lives and very few have even thus escaped.

"Wherever they go, the mark of Cain is on them and their lives are forfeited and it is made the duty of any good Mormon to take their lives wherever they find them. It is held that if their blood is shed, it will ascend unto heaven as a sacrifice for their sins and will atone for their sins, and they will be saved. "It is also taught, that the blood of Joseph Smith, is upon this generation and that the Saints are especially charged to avenge his blood on the people of the United States. That if any one in authority persecutes "the Saints," his life is forfeited and it is the duty of any Saint to "cut off" such a person. If, therefore, there is any move made in Congress, the traveling Elder, our representative and the newspapers and the resident brethren combine their efforts and by threats or bribes, defeat any unfriendly laws." "I was astonished beyond measure at these revelations, and no longer wonder at the abject obedience to Brigham's sovereign will. How long will these things be and not arouse the indignation of a duped and outraged government.'"

CHAPTER XIX.

WE VISIT THE HAREM.

From Mrs. Burlingame's Journal.

I had now been in Salt Lake City nearly a year and had become well acquainted with the Mormon women. I had met a number of Brigham's wives and had visited at the house of Mrs. Cobb, but I had never been through the Harem, or seen the women "at home." I wanted very much to do so and one day a lady who had been one of Brigham's wives, said if I would dress up as a "sister" just come in with the last emigration, she would go with me and visit the Harem. We went up early in the day and the women were generally engaged in their own apartments in attending to their own rooms and their own children's clothing.

We entered the parlor and found ourselves in a long narrow room, with a large window in front, and four on the side, all heavily curtained. A beautiful Brussels carpet, design, a large boquet of flowers, a rose, surrounded with other flowers and leaves with a light ground, covers the floor. Two center-tables of solid Mahogony, are placed at equal distances from the ends of the room. An elegant rose-wood piano sits at the lower end of the room. Between the windows hangs a large mirror, under which is a melodeon. A large sofa, upholstered with crimson velvet occupies the opposite side, and near this is a bureau, with silver candle-sticks, and other ornaments. The chairs are painted to represent Mahogony, and are gilded. The room is gilded. A large stove in the corner near the door, completes the furniture of the drawing room of the Harem.

The family meet in this room, every morning and evening at the ringing of the bell, to attend family prayers. From this we passed into No. 2 which Mrs. Emeline Free occupies. She has long been the reigning favorite, the "light of the Harem." The furniture in this room consists of a three ply-carpet, a high post bedstead, with white and red curtains, sofa, table, chairs painted to resemble oak, a large square mirror, oil shades, wardrobe and fire place. It is here that the Prophet formerly spent much of his time, reaching the room by a private hall to avoid the jealousy of the other wives. Emeline dressed his curls, petted and caressed him, and worshiped him alternately as her God.

She received us kindly and bade us be seated. She is tall and graceful; with mild violet eyes, fair wavy hair and has that dreamy style of beauty which is so captivating to men. She would suggest those exquisite lines in Lalla Rooke.

> ——"O Nourmahal;
> Thou loveliest, dearest of them all;
> The one whose smile shone out alone
> Amidst a world, the only one
> Whose light, among so many lights,
> Was like that star, on starry nights,
> The seaman singles from the sky,
> To steer his bark forever by."

Mr. and Mrs. Free were opposed to polygamy, and Brigham went one day to convince them of their error. The beautiful Emeline was the first he sought to win, and he argued and expounded the new doctrine with wonderful zeal and fervor. At length the parents were convinced. The Prophet of the Lord stepped up to Emeline, laid his saintly hand upon her shoulder, and said, in fervid accents, "Emeline, will you be my wife?" "Yes sir," was the reply. This was their courtship. She at once became the favorite, and many a heart grew sad when she became an inmate of the Harem.

Brigham distinguished her in every way; gave her better rooms than the rest, and servants to wait upon her. She grew to love him, and obtained a powerful influence over him. There is no weapon so powerful as a woman's tears. This Emeline believed, and often acted upon, to bring back her truant lover, when she thought too much attention was paid to others. Finally, so great became the jealousy of the other wives, that the husband of these contending fair ones constructed a private hall leading from his office to Emeline's room, that he might visit her without observation or constraint. He devoted himself to her exclusively, and she reigned supreme over the sisters. She received her company in the grand saloon; she occupied the seat of honor at the table, at the right hand of her husband. In short, she was the mistress of the Harem.

At that time the most of the women did their own work, and staid in their own rooms, so that there was but little communication with each other. She has eight children, but is still a young-looking woman.

After a pleasant chat with this lovely woman, we took our leave and continued our calls among the women.

No. 3. Mrs. Cobb formerly occupied this room, but now resides in a neat cottage outside the walls. A three ply carpet, red and yellow, common bedstead standing in a recess, fall-leaf table, chairs painted oak, oil-shades with white curtains, a small mirror, also a small closet and fireplace, constitute the furniture of this room. This was the home of a woman who had lived in a comfortable and commodious house in Boston, as its mistress and head, with a large and interesting family around her. All this she left for the ridiculous delusion called Mormonism. To what extremes will not religious fanaticism and mistaken zeal lead its devotees!

No. 4 is a large, pleasant room, with bedroom attached. This was occupied by Clara Chase and her children, before her death. She was once a favorite with Brigham, which will account for her superior accommodations. This room is furnished as follows: a carpet similar to Emeline's, common bedstead placed in a recess, common table, nice large gilt mirror, red and white curtains, wardrobe, and fireplace.

No. 5. This room, opposite the parlor, belongs to Lucy Decker, the first wife in plurality, and is rather plainly furnished. Rag-carpet, plain bedstead, stand, mirror, oak chairs, wardrobe, small cupboard and a fireplace, curtains of the prevailing colors red and white. A sitting-room and two bedrooms are allowed Mrs. Lucy Decker, as she has a number of children.

No. 6. In Clara Decker's room stands a beautifully carved bedstead, arched overhead with heavy damask curtains, chairs like parlor, stand, settee, Venetian blinds, and oil-shades. Brigham's portrait in oil, half size, hangs on the wall, also a large mirror. A rag-carpet covers the floor. A bedroom and recess are attached to this room, and from its superior furniture it is easy to infer that its occupant is a woman fond of show, as well as a favorite with the Prophet.

No. 7. Lucy Bigelow's room contains a common bedstead, three chairs, a stand, wardrobe, carpet, mirror, and white curtains.

No. 8. Hall leading to Emeline's room.

No. 9. Emily Partridge, one of the "proxies," occupies this room. A common carpet, calico curtains, a fall-leaf table, bedstead and the usual quota of chairs, make up the furniture of this woman's home.

Formerly, a tin pail and tin wash-dish constituted the toilet set of most of the wives, but since the Prophet has had so many fat government contracts, and his purse has become plethoric with public money, and from the continued inflow of tithing, he has indulged his "women folks" with crockery ware. As Uncle Sam is rich, and a good easy-going soul, why should he not furnish "Harems" for his "loyal and law abiding citizens?"

No. 10 is Aunt Fanny Murray's room. Her furniture consists of a red and yellow carpet, home-made bedsteads, oak chairs, a fall-leaf table, and oil-shades. A sitting-room and a small bedroom belong to Aunt Fanny. But you ask, Who is Aunt Fanny? She was in her young days, Fanny Young, and had a great awkward brother called Brigham. She married a Mr. Murray, to whom she was devotedly attached. She was a gentle, kind creature; and when her husband died, she became dependent on her brother. She had long been a believer in Mormonism, and was with the Mormons at Nauvoo. After the death of her husband, she was, by the earnest persuasion of her brother Brigham, induced to be sealed to another. She protested at the time, and said it would break her heart. And in relating the story to a young friend, years afterward,—"Bessie," said she, "my poor, poor heart is breaking now;" and laying her hand on her heart, she wept aloud. Aunt Fanny has gone to her rest. She has suffered want and privation, mental anguish and bodily pain, for her religion. . Who shall say that her dear heavenly Father, whom she so blindly worshiped, will not reward her with a crown of glory in His kingdom above, when she shall rejoin the partner of her youth, free from the shackles of tyranny and superstition?

Nos. 11 and 12 are staircases.

No. 13. Main Hall, extending the whole length of the building; it is lighted from a large window at the further end.

This completes the principal story of the Lion House.

THE BASEMENT STORY.—No. 14. General cellar, where all kinds of vegetables and provisions are stored.

No. 15. Ash-house.

No. 16. Weaving-room. The wives spin, color, and prepare the yarn, and a man is kept employed in weaving. A large quantity of cloth is made at the Harem every year. Brigham's motto is, "No drones in the hive."

No. 17 is the coachman's room.

No. 18. Pantry. Milk, pies, cake, bread, and cooked provisions are kept in this place.

No. 19. Back Hall.

No. 20 was formerly occupied as a schoolroom and dancing academy for the Youngs.

No. 21. Wash-room.

No. 22. Kitchen.

No. 23. Dish-room.

No. 24. The Dining-room is about fifteen by forty feet. Two tables extend its whole length, allowing only a passage-way at each end. A third table extends two thirds of the length of the room. Also a side-table, and chairs of different sizes, to accommodate the various ages of the family group.

Each wife has her seat at the table, and her children sit with her. The wives who have children are seated at the heads of the tables in the order in which they came into the family,—they taking the preference over those who have no children. This is the case in every well-regulated Mormon family. Among Mormons, the title of mother includes that of queen, and is consequently the highest distinction a woman can attain. If a woman has no childrhn, she is miserable, and her position in society is a very unpleasant one. She can only redeem herself by urging her husband to take more wives. Many women do this, and afterward labor incessantly for the new mistresses and their children.

Lucy Decker, the first "plurality" woman, presides at one of the long tables. At the head of the short table, Brigham always presides, when he takes his meals at the Harem. On his right sits Clara Decker, with her children, and on the left, Emeline, with hers. This order is strictly observed. This preference causes much unhappiness on the part of other wives less favored.

No. 25. Main Hall.
No. 26 and 27 are staircases.
No. 28. Small side Hall.

THIRD STORY.—This floor is divided in the centre by a wide hall, and ranged on either side are ten small rooms, of nearly uniform size, with one door and window each. These rooms are about twelve by fifteen feet, and are occupied principally by those of the women who have no children. The windows are of the Gothic style.

No. 29 is occupied by "Twiss," and has a carpet, common bedstead, three oak chairs, a little toilet stand, small mirror, and plain white curtains.

All these rooms are similarly furnished. All are neat and clean. Harriet Cook, Ellen Rockwood, and Twiss, display more taste than the others in the arrangement of their little cages.

In addition to these articles, Harriet Cook has mahogany chairs, instead of oak, and a large cupboard, painted to represent mahogany. All the rooms are furnished with stoves, except three, which have fireplaces.

No books, except the Book of Mormon, Book of Doctrine and Covenants, and Mormon Hymn-Book, will be seen in any room except Eliza Snow's; she being a woman of considerable literary taste, and withal a writer,—having made a number of contributions to Mormon literature,—her room is indicative of the same, being well supplied with books and papers.

What the women do.

The internal arrangement of affairs at the Harem is very similar to that of a young ladies boarding-school. Each woman having her own room, her affairs are all centered there. The culinary department is under the control of such of the wives as Brigham from time to time appoints. She is the stewardess, and carries the keys. A cook is employed,—generally a man,—and several servants besides, who are all under the control of the stewardess.

When the meals are prepared and ready, the bell rings, and each woman, with her children, if she have any, files down to the dinner-table, and is seated as before stated.

Each, on rising, has her children to attend to and get ready for breakfast; this over, she commences the business of the day, arranges her rooms, and sits down to her sewing or other work, as the case may be.

A sewing-machine is brought into requisition, and one of the number appointed to use it. For the benefit of those who want a sewing-machine, it may be well to state how this one was procured. One day a man from St. Louis came to offer one for sale, stating that his price was ninety dollars. Brigham bought it, promising to pay the man whenever he should call. The man being poor, called in a few days. He did not get his pay. He called again, a number of times with the same result. One of the wives became quite indignant, and said,—"If I was in his place, 1 never would ask it of one so high in the priesthood. He had better give it to him than to ask pay of him." The poor man never received his money, and as soon as he could get the means, left the Territory. This is the manner in which the Prophet becomes possessed of much of his property.

Most of the women spin and make their every-day clothing, doing their own coloring. They are quite proud of the quantity of cloth manufactured in their establishment every year. All work hard, and take but very little out-of-door exercise. Parties and the theatre are the favorite amusements. At the theater, Brigham and one or two of the favored wives sit together in the "King's box," but the remainder of the women and children sit in what is called "Brigham's corral." This is in the parquette, about the center of the area. The Prophet goes down once or twice during the evening to the corral, and chats for a few moments with one and another, but in a short time he can be seen beside his "dear Amelia" again.

At the Mormon parties, much gayety prevails. Appearances are maintained, somewhat, by paying more respectful deference to the first wives, on such occasions. Gentiles, with whom the saints are on good terms, are well received and kindly entertained at these parties, and all join in giving themselves up to the influence of mirth and festivity. Dancing is not only a favorite amusement, it is more; it is cultivated to such an extent that it becomes a passion.

Brigham's women, though better clothed than formerly, still work very hard. They are infatuated with their religion, and devoted to their husband. If they cannot obtain his love, they content themselves with his kindness, and endeavor to think themselves happy. As religion is their only solace, they try to make it their only object. If it does not elevate their minds, it deadens their susceptibilities, and as they are not permitted to be WOMEN, they try to convince themselves that it is God's will they should be SLAVES.

A music-master, a dancing-master, and a teacher of the ordinary branches of an English education, are employed in the family school. Also a teacher of French. His children have much better advantages than any other in the Territory. Dancing and music are the leading accomplishments, and everything else is made subordinate to these.

We passed a very pleasant morning, and after inspecting the house and the domestic arrangements, we took a walk through the gardens and grounds. Here utility was, as in the Mansion, made the leading feature. Nothing was done simply for show. Choice fruits, such as the peach, the pear, the apricot and plum were in profusion, and currants, strawberries and other small fruit were plenty. Vegetables were abundant and of excellent quality. Each wife had a little parterre of flowers, mostly of the old fashioned kind, marigolds, honey suckles and hollyhocks and peonies, and scattered everywhere and perfuming the whole garden, were numerous bushes of the flowering currant which grows wild and luxuriantly in these mountains.

There is no more lovely scene than the grounds of the "Prophet's Block," sloping as they do towards the south and covered with all their wealth of fruits and flowers. My friend, who had lived in the Prophet's family and is perfectly familiar with everything connected therewith, said she would give me a description of all of the wives some day when we both had leisure.

CHAPTER XX.

THE WIVES OF THE PROPHET.
From Mrs. Burlingame's Journal.

Yesterday according to appointment, my friend came over and said if agreeable she would redeem her promise. Said she, "You will naturally want to know about Mrs. Mary Ann Angell Young, the first living and legal wife of the Prophet."

She is a native of New York, and is a fine looking, intelligent woman. She is large, portly, and dignified. Her hair is well sprinkled with the frosts of age; her clear, hazel eyes and melancholy countenance indicate a soul where sorrow reigns supreme. She has been very much attached to her husband, and his infidelity has made deep inroads upon her mind. Her deepseated melancholy often produces flights of insanity, which increase with her declining years.

Bereft of her husband's society, she naturally clings to her children, of whom she has five: Joseph, Brigham A., John, Alice and Luna. They all reside with her. She formerly occupied the "Bee Hive House," but as the number of her husband's wives increased, it became necessary that additional accommodations should be furnished the "plural" portion of the family. The first wife was obliged to vacate her residence for the benefit of new comers. She was removed to a great barn-like house on the hill. This building looks more like a penitentiary than anything else. It was the first house built upon the premises, and, as before stated, is very deficient in the number and size of its windows.

Mrs. Young seldom receives guests, and her husband himself, scarcely ever pays her a visit.

When I looked upon this poor, suffering woman, as she sat at church, surrounded by her husband's mistresses, I seemed for the first time fully to realize the true character of that "institution" which has crushed the hearts of many noble women.

She is very kind to her children and dependents, and is much beloved by them. She has not succeeded so well in gaining the affection of "the wives." With them she is very unpopular, and by some of them she is often mocked and upbraided. It is said, "one hates whom he has injured." This may account for much of this feeling among the "plurals."

Joseph, or Joe Young, as he is familiarly known in Utah, is a fast young man. He has been on a "mission," travelled in Europe, smokes, chews, gets drunk, swears, preaches the gospel, has three wives whom he whips and otherwise shamefully abuses, and is a good Mormon, in full fellowship in the church. While at a fashionable watering place, at Great Salt Lake, in the summer of 1863, he insulted a gentile lady. The gentleman who accompanied her being an officer, promptly knocked him down, and this not seeming to be satisfactory, afterwards challenged him. Joseph's friends interfered and obtained a settlement of the difficulty.

Brigham A. is more respectable. He has also been on a "mission." This is equivalent to saying that he has been wild and reckless, as it is the Mormon custom to send all who are unruly and hard to manage, or who have committed crimes, on a mission. It is thought that by "bearing the pure vessels of the Lord" to such poor, wicked wretches as the gentiles, they will perchance themselves become purified.

John, being the youngest, has not developed his tastes so fully. He seems inclined to seek after the loaves and fishes of office. He was Serjeant-at Arms of the Council in the winter of 1863–64, and will doubtless be a member when he is old enough, should his father then reign in Utah.

Mrs. Alice Clawson is the oldest daughter. Rather amiable, with fair hair, blue eyes, and small in stature. She is one of the performers in her father's theatre. As an *artiste*, she is "flat, stale and unprofitable." But being Brigham's daughter and good looking, she is applauded to the echo. She is one of three wives of Hiram B. Clawson, who is the Prophet's chief business agent and manager. Quick, shrewd and unscrupulous, he is a fit instrument with which to accomplish the purposes of such a man.

In the year 1851, a Mr. Tobin came to Salt Lake with Captain Stansbury. While there he met Miss Alice, fell in love with her, and they were engaged to be married. Mr. T. had occasion to leave Salt Lake on business, and did not return until 1856. He then renewed his engagement with Alice, but afterward, for reasons satisfactory to himself, broke it. This subjected him to the vengeance of her father, which never slumbers. Tobin and his party were followed, attacked in the night, on Santa Clara River, 370 miles south of Salt Lake City. Several of the party were severely wounded. They lost six horses and were compelled to abandon their baggage, which was completely riddled by bullets. During Tobin's absence, Alice had been engaged to another, who had been sent off to the Sandwich Islands, by her watchful father. Hiram B. Clawson, the confidential clerk of the President, next appeared as a candidate for the young lady's hand. He had already one wife, but was anxious to secure a second.

A little incident in their courtship, will illustrate the manner of obtaining No. 2.

"Good morning, sister Clawson," said a young friend whom she met in walking.

"What do you wish me to understand?"

"Nothing more than that your father gave his consent this morning, in my presence, to your marriage with Hiram Clawson."

"This matter begins to be serious," said Alice, "now that my father has given me away to a man that has one wife already, and is courting another beside me, both of them much handsomer than I am."

Hiram was nettled, for it was true that he was

courting a third wife, and of the three Alice was the least beautiful, She then proposed, playfully, to elope with an old gentleman, a friend of the family. "I would do so" she said, "before I would be given away like an old mule, to a man who already has one wife, and is seeking for others."

Yet Alice, though doubtless giving expression to the sentiments of her heart, was afterwards prevailed upon, and consented to become No. 2 in the harem of Hiram B. Clawson. Hiram having commenced at a much earlier age than his father-in-law, may, if unchecked in his career, yet rival him in the number of his wives and the extent and magnificence of his "plural" establishment.

Luna Young is a character. She is very wilful and headstrong. She always governed her sister Alice, and even her father could not control this wayward child.

She is the fourth daughter by the first wife, two having died. She has light hair, blue eyes and a fair complexion. She is very haughty and beautiful. Slender as the gazelle, and free and joyous as a bird, brooking no control, she was the light, and often the annoyance of her father's house in her girlish days. She is now married and very likely will become amiable and docile, under Mormon discipline.

Lucy Decker Seely is the first wife in "plurality,"—or the second "woman."

Lucy Decker was married to Isaac Seely and had two children. She afterward became a Mormon and went to Nauvoo to reside. Her husband, Seely, was somewhat dissipated, but treated her well. She, however, saw Brother Brigham and loved him. He visited her, told her that Seely could never give her an "exaltation" in the eternal world; that he, being high in the priesthood, could make her a queen in the first resurrection.

She yielded to these inducements and the promptings of her inclination, left her husband, and was sealed to Brigham Young.

Lucy Decker has brown hair, dark eyes, small features, a fair skin and of short stature; but quite *en bon point*. She would strongly remind you of a New-England housewife, "fat, fair and forty." In common with nearly all the inmates of the Harem, she is of very ordinary intellect and limited education.

Her first child, after marrying Young, was named Brigham Heber, and was the first born in Mormon polygamy. He is now a lad of about eighteen years of age.

Lucy Decker is still one of the favorite wives. She lives in the Bee Hive and keeps a sort of boarding house for the work hands. She has had eight children by Brigham, all of whom are living. A story is told which illustrates well the disposition and character of these polygamous children. Brigham Heber was in the habit of playing while the family were at breakfast. One morning, after breakfast was over, this boy, then only ten or twelve years of age, went into the kitchen and undertook to help himself to anything he could find. Mr. Smith, the cook, would not permit it. Brigham Heber seized a fork and, with oaths that would put a pirate to shame, swore he would stab the cook. Smith caught him, wrenched the fork from his hand and pushed him into the hall. He and Oscar, son of Harriet Cook, swore they would kill Smith the first time they should catch him out.

Clara Decker, sister of Lucy Decker, is a short, thick-set person, very much like Lucy in appearance. She is much more intelligent and agreeable than her sister, and in every way her superior. She is also quite a favorite with the Prophet; has three or four children, and is much attached to her "husband."

Harriet Cook was early in plurality; having been sealed to Brigham, at "Winter Quarters," on the Missouri River, while the Mormons were on their way to Utah. This was five years before polygamy was publicly proclaimed in Utah as a divine institution. Harriet is very tall, has light hair, blue eyes, a fair complexion and sharp nose. She is rather slender, but has much power of endurance and a look of determination.

When all is going on smoothly, she is as calm and serene as a May morning; but let Brigham or any one else in the establishment cross her path, and the blue eyes at once light up and give evidence of a coming storm. When irritated and aroused, she denounces the whole Mormon religion, including polygamy, and says, "the whole thing is a humbug and may go to the devil for all she cares." Brigham, though a stern disciplinarian, makes good his escape, at such times, and the 'women' all keep at a respectful distance.

When she is in a religious mood, which is seldom the case, she says, "I don't profess to know much, but there is one thing I do understand, and that is Mormonism. Whenever Brother Brigham, (all the wives call him Brother,) goes behind the veil, I make him tell me what he sees and hears there. I mean to know all about it." She is the smartest of all the women. She has one son in plurality, named Oscar. He is a wild, ugly boy and curses his mother *ad libitum*. Brigham cares nothing for this woman and avoids her as much as possible.

Lucy Bigelow is of middling stature, has dark brown hair, blue eyes, aquiline nose and a pretty mouth, and is very pleasant and affable. She is very pretty and ladylike in the ball room, but does not appear to so good advantage in the nursery or kitchen. She is the one who was the subject of a well-turned repartee at the anniversary ball in Salt Lake City, on the 24th of July, 1863.

Governor Harding, having danced with several of the wives of "Governor" Young, became somewhat enthusiastic and extravagant in his compliments, and among other fine sayings he remarked to one of the wives, upon leading her on to the floor, "The President has introduced several of his wives to me as 'Mrs. Young,' 'Mrs. Young,' 'Mrs. Young.' As well might the astronomer point me to the stars of heaven, without giving me their names." "Governor, I understand your compliment and appreciate it, The name of this particular star is Lucy."

She has but little influence over Brigham, and he seldom visits her.

Twiss has sandy hair, inclined to curl, round features, blue eyes, low forehead, complexion fair, face somewhat freckled. She is short and stout. This woman makes a good servant and is always ready to wait on her lord and master. She prepares his linen and is content.

Martha Bowker is low in stature, with black hair and eyes. She is very quiet. Is plain and sensible; neither showy nor interesting. Very neat in dress, very ordinary in intellect and acquirements. She is of few words and rather quick tempered. Very little influence over the Prophet.

Harriet Barney is tall, slender and graceful. She has hazel eyes, light brown hair, mild, sweet expression of countenance, and is indeed a lovely woman. Her character is as beautiful as her face, and the suffering and sorrowing always find a friend in her. She is patient and forbearing, and would rather suffer wrong than do wrong. Her kind and sympathetic nature and excellent character, place her far above all the other inmates of the Harem.

Believing in polygamy, she left her husband, and became one of the plural wives of the President of the church in which she believed. She loves, with all the intensity of her nature, him for whom she has sacrificed everything. Of course, she deeply feels his neglect, but, like a true woman, complains not. Having sacrificed her happiness upon the altar of her faith, she continues to love, to endure and to suffer.

She had three children by her first husband; none since.

The parents of Eliza Burgess resided in Manchester, England, and came to Nauvoo in the early days of Mormonism. Soon after, they both died, leaving Eliza an orphan. She was thrown upon the cold charities of the world, and Brother Brigham, ever the friend of youth and beauty, took her into his family. She served seven years and then desired to marry another. She applied to Young for his consent, but the Prophet had other projects inconsistent in their nature with the proposed marriage. "Eliza," he said, "you have been so long in the family that I need you. I wish to marry you myself. Will you not be my wife? Brother S. is a very good man, but I can give you a greater exaltation. I can make you a queen." This argument was conclusive, Eliza gave up her lover and married Brigham Young.

In person Eliza is small, with large dark eyes, dark hair and dark complexion. She is quick tempered and is of the class—English servant girl. She is the only one of the Prophet's women who is not an American. She has several children.

Ellen Rockwood is of medium size, slender, with light hair, light brown eyes and fair complexion. She is the daughter of the warden of the penitentiary, who is a regular down east

Yankee. Ellen is rather quiet, even tempered, but quite narrow minded. Her health is poor and she spends most of her time in embroidery and needlework. She has no children and per consequence, very little influence with her husband. He calls upon her in her little room, about once in six months.

Susan Snively is a middle aged woman, of medium size, dark hair, light eyes, dark complexion and expressionless face; the plainest of all the women. She is good and kind in her nature, quiet and retiring. She spins and colors yarn, and is a good housewife, of the type—New England farmer's wife. Having no children, she adds nothing to the kingdom and glory of her husband, and is estimated accordingly.

Jemima Angell is the sister of Mary Ann, the lawful wife. She is an elderly lady, with dark hair, grey eyes and pensive countenance. Of low stature, but quite robust. Her first husband died out of the church and she is merely sealed to Young, for her exaltation in another state. She lives in a little house by herself, and seldom receives a visit from her spiritual husband.

· Margaret Alley is short and small; light hair and eyes, rather lengthened features, but mild expression of countenance. Being much neglected by her husband, she became very melancholy,

She died in 1853, leaving two children.

Margaret Pierce is of medium height, light hair, and blue eyes, sharp nose and very variable in temper. She has several children, but not much influence with her husband.

Mrs. Hampton is very tall and noble in appearance, has round features, large, lustrous eyes, dark hair and fair complexion. She was early married to Mr. Hampton, by whom she had six children. They removed to Nauvoo, where Hampton died. Mrs. Hampton was afterward sealed to Young.

When the Mormons were driven from Nauvoo, Mrs. Hampton was for some reason left behind. She then married a Mr. Cole, by whom she had one daughter, named Vilate. When this child was about four years old, Cole went to California. Young then sent for Mrs. Hampton to come and live with him. She obeyed, and became a second time one of his plural wives. During this time Cole wrote letters frequently and sent her his likeness.

About this time, Feramorz Little, one of Young's nephews, married Julia Hampton, the daughter of Mrs. H. and half sister to Vilate Cole. Mrs. Hampton lived at the Harem about eight years and superintended the culinary department. Some misunderstanding having arisen between her and the Prophet, he again cast her off. It is said that she was unwilling to be sealed over the altar for eternity to Young, preferring her first husband in the eternal world.

Vilate is now about fourteen years old, beautiful and accomplished. She and Brigham Heber were engaged to be married, but his father disapproved the match and laid a plan to defeat it. In the fall of 1863, Feramorz Little sent for Vilate to come down to the city, and proposed to have her board with him and attend school. His real object was to secure her for his fourth wife and at the same time prevent her marrying the son of the President. During all this time the girl frequently inquired, with much anxiety, about her father.

In 1863, Cole enlisted in the 2d Regiment of Infantry, Nevada Volunteers, and came to Salt Lake City expressly for the purpose of finding his daughter. After much inquiry, he ascertained where his wife and child were living and wrote a letter to Vilate. The mother received the letter, read it and put it into the fire. Thus the matter rested, until Vilate came into the city. One day she said to her sister Julia, (Mrs. Little,) "Would it not be strange if my father was among the soldiers?" Said Julia, "He is. Didn't you know it? Nephi told me all about it." This gave her new courage, and thenceforth she made every effort to see her father. For some time she was closely watched and Cole, who had found where she was, was denied admission to her; but the girl's resolution remaining firm, Little fearing she would leave him, finally permitted an interview. The happy meeting of the father with his only child, after an absence of eleven years, who shall describe? Cole still remains in Utah, devoted to his daughter, whom he visits frequently, and is not without hope of getting her away from her unfortunate associations. The task is a delicate and difficult one, and in his efforts to accomplish it he has the sympathy of every father.

Mary Bigelow was sealed to Young at "Winter Quarters," and came on with him to Utah. After a time she left the Harem, and what became of her is unknown.

PROXY WOMEN.

This is a common term in Utah. and signifies that a woman is married to one man for "time," and sealed to another for eternity.

All her children belong to the man to whom she is sealed, no matter which may be their father, or whether the mother ever married the celestial husband in "time." This is a refinement upon the Jewish doctrine, which required a man to "raise up children to his dead brother."

Of this class of women Brigham Young has four, all of whom, while they live with him for "time," are sealed to Joseph Smith for eternity, and to Joseph must they be delivered over, with their children, in the first resurrection.

Miss Eliza Roxy Snow is of middling stature, dark hair, well silvered with gray; dark eyes, noble, intelligent countenance and quiet, dignified manner. She is the most intellectual of the women.

Her literary taste and acquirements are good, and she has composed some very creditable hymns for the church of which she is a conscientious and devoted member. A volume of her poems has also been published, some of which evince genius of a high order.

She is quite exclusive in her tastes and associates but little with the women. She occupies a small room on the third floor of the Harem, about twelve by fifteen feet in size. A neat carpet covers the floor; a common bedstead occupies one corner. There are some oak chairs grained, with crochet covers. white window-curtains and bedspread, her "own handiwork." Behind the door is a neat little wardrobe. On a shelf over the window stands a vase of artificial flowers. A stand, covered with books, usually occupies the centre of the room, and these articles, with a neat little stove, make up the furniture.

This is the home of "the sweet singer of Israel." She has cast the charm of her genius over the rude materials, and there is an air of comfort, neatness and refinement about her little sanctum which is not apparent in any other portion of the house. Here she receives and entertains her company. She occupies her time chiefly in writing, and in needle work. She is highly respected by the family, who call her "one of the nobles of the earth." When tired of writing and study, she walks out and visits her friends. If any one is sick in the house she looks after the invalid and shows every kindness and attention. She soothes the afflicted and cares for the infirm and aged. She and Zina D. Huntington are the most lady like and accomplished of the wives.

The following verses, written by Eliza R. Snow will show her style, as well as the religious fervor and fanaticism for which she is remarkable.

For the *Deseret News*.
"*The Ladies of Utah, to the Ladies of the Umited States Camp, in Crusade against the Mormons.*

MISS ELIZA R. SNOW.

Why are you in these mountains,
Exposed to frosts and snows?
Far from your sheltering houses,
From comfort and repose?

Has cruel persecution,
  With unrelenting hand,
Thrust you from home and kindred,
  And from your native land?

Have you been robbed and plundered,
  Till you are penniless,
And then in destitution
  Driven to the wilderness?

No, no; you've joined a crusade
  Against the peace of those
Driven to these distant valleys
  By cruel, murderous foes.

Amid the dreary desert,
  Where hideous red men roam;
Where beasts of prey were howling,
  We've made ourselves a home.

Can woman's heart be callous,
  And made of flint and steel?
Perhaps you'll learn to pity,
  When you are made to *feel*.

Should sickness prey upon you,
  And children cry for bread,
With bitter self-reproaches
  You'll rue the path you tread.

We love with purest feelings,
  Our husbands, children, friends;
We've learned to prize the blessings
  Which God in mercy sends.

We have the ancient order
  To us by prophets given,
And here we have the pattern
  As things exist in heaven.

> We'd fain from human suffering
> Each barbed arrow draw,
> But yet self-preservation
> Is God's and Nature's law.
>
> The Scriptures are fulfilling,
> The spoiler's being spoiled;
> All Satan's foul devices
> 'Gainst Zion will be foiled.
>
> *Great Salt Lake City, Oct. 13, 1857."*

Zina D. Huntingdon Jacobs is of large form well proportioned, high forehead, with light hair and eyes. She is of a melancholy temperament, as is plainly indicated by the expression of her countenance. She has three children and has charge of the children of Clara Chase.

Zina has some literary ability, and sometimes writes poetry. She has a special office in the family which is to act as governess for all the young ladies, accompanying them in their attendance to singing schools and other public places. Zina came to Utah with her husband, Dr. Jacobs. Young became attached to her, sent the Doctor on a mission, and in his absence appropriated to himself the wife and children. Dr. Jacobs is still in California, and is an "apostate." Zina stands in great awe of Brigham, who treats her with marked coldness and neglect.

Amelia Partridge is rather tall, with a fine form, black hair, dark eyes, dark complexion, sweet expression of countenance, and very mild and amiable in disposition. She and her sister Eliza had been servants in the family of Joseph Smith, in Nauvoo.

Amelia has four children, to whom she is devotedly attached. She is a kind and gentle mother, patient and forgiving, one of the excellent ones of earth. She takes but little interest in family matters, outside of the circle of her own children.

Mrs. Augusta Cobb is a native of Massachusetts, and formerly resided in Boston. She is a large, fine-looking person, dark hair, gray eyes and clear complexion. She is very stylish in appearance and of dignified demeanor. She was converted to Mormonism at Boston, fifteen years ago, left her husband and a very interesting family of children, and with one little girl, Charlotte, came to Utah and took up her residence at the Harem, as a plural wife of Brigham Young.

She is high spirited and imperious. She once returned to her family in Boston and remained two years, but was too deeply involved in the meshes of Mormonism to be satisfied away from Zion, and again returned to Salt Lake. She now lives in a neat little cottage near the Lion House and is supported by Young. Her son, James Cobb, after finishing his course of study in the East, came to Salt Lake, and after some years, through the influence of his mother, joined the church. Previous to becoming a Mormon, he expressed much anxiety about his mother and sister Charlotte, now an interesting young lady, and used many arguments and entreaties to induce them to leave, but finally himself yielded to the seductive influences which surrounded him.

Mrs. Smith is an elderly woman who admired Brother Brigham very much and desired to be sealed to him, to insure her salvation. Young did not reciprocate her sentiments toward him, but compromised the matter by sealing her to Joseph Smith for eternity, and to himself for time. After this ceremony had been performed, he committed her to the care of the Bishop of the ward directing him to support her.

There are many of this class of women in the Territory.

Clara Chase was of medium height, dark hair and eyes, rather sullen expression of countenance, low forehead and features indicative of deep-seated melancholy. When Young married her, he treated her with marked consideration. He assigned to her an elegant apartment, in which hung the only oil painting of himself. She from the first distrusted the principle of polygamy, and had many misgivings of conscience in regard to her course in marrying the Prophet.

For a time she lived in this way, in a strait between two opinions. When her husband treated her kindly, she tried to be happy, but when he was cold and unfeeling toward her, she was driven well-nigh to desperation. In the mean time she had four children, two of whom are now living. They are bright and intelligent girls, fourteen and sixteen years of age.

As she approached her fourth confinement her fits of remorse became more frequent and more terrible. She repreached herself with having committed the unpardonable sin. Her condition was truly pitiable. During her sickness Brigham treated her with so much coldness and neglect that she became actually insane and raved incessantly,—"Oh, I have committed the unpardonable sin! Oh, warn my poor children not to follow my bad example. I am going to hell. Brigham has caused it. Oh! do not any of you go into polygamy. It will curse you and damn your souls eternally." When her husband appeared, she cursed him as the author of her destruction.

The "President" and his two "counsellors" "laid hands" on her, but all of no avail. Dr. Sprague, the family physician, was sent for; but her poor wrecked spirit would no longer abide where it had suffered so much, and she died a raving maniac.

Amelia Folsom is a native of Portsmouth, N. H. She is tall and well formed, with light hair, grey eyes and regular features She is quite pale, owing to ill health. Has but little refinement of manner. When at the theatre, sitting in the King's box, with her husband, the observed of all observers, she may be seen eating apples, throwing the skins about, chatting with Brigham and occasionally levelling her glass at some one in the assembly.

She plays and sings, but with indifferent skill, and taste. She was, for a long time, unwilling to marry the President, but he continued his suit with a pertinacity worthy of a better cause, and by repeated promises of advancement made to herself and her parents, finally succeeded. For several months he had urged his suit, during which time his carriage might be seen, almost any day, standing at her father's door, for hours at a time. He told her she was created expressly for himself and could marry no one else on pain of everlasting destruction. She pleaded, protested and wept, but he persevered, and at length, when all other arguments failed, he told her he had received a special revelation from

Heaven on the subject. She had always believed in Mormonism, and had been taught to have faith in revelation. "Amelia," he said, "you must be my wife; God has revealed it to me. You cannot be saved by any one else. If you marry me I will save you and exalt you to be a queen in the celestial world, but if you refuse, you will be destroyed, both soul and body.

The poor girl believed this hellish imposter, and yielding to his wishes, became his wife. For several months after her marriage, Amelia was sad and dejected, but of late she has rallied and now appears the gayest of the gay. This marriage took place on the 29th of January, 1863, more than six months after the passage by Congress of the anti-polygamy law, and was public and notorious. Here was perpetrated, in one act, the double crime of destroying forever the happiness of a young lady and setting before his people the example of an open violation of the law of the land. Yet for both crimes he goes unpunished and continues to sit in his chair of state, clothed in authority and power, not only the wonder, but the admiration, of thousands outside of the Mormon church!

Amelia is evidently living under constraint and acting an assumed character. She is playing the *role* of a happy wife, with a breaking heart.

At the time of her marriage, her heart had been given to another, to whom she should have been married. That she compromised her character, in marrying Young under the circumstances, is a fact too notorious to be concealed, and this connection has brought more odium upon polygamy than any the President ever formed.

Nevertheless, Amelia stands the recognized Queen of the Harem. She leads the fashion, and is the model woman for the saints. Thousands bow low as she passes, and think themselves happy to receive her passing recognition. She is now a queen and is to be a goddess in the celestial world. The new wife sometimes becomes restive and impatient, and treats her liege lord rather shabbily. She is at times notional and imperious and somewhat coquettish, to all of which her husband submits with good grace for the present and pets her as a child.

The Bee Hive House, formerly occupied by Mrs. Young and her family, has been vacated for Amelia. Servants are at her disposal and her establishment is extensive and imposing.

Brigham spends much of his time with his new wife and often dines with her. One evening a friend was taking tea with the newly-married couple. Amelia behaved quite naughtily toward her lord. After tea was finished, they remained at the table, eating nuts and confectioneries. Amelia threw her shells through an open window, on the other side of the room. Her husband said, "Amelia, don't do that; put your shells by your plate." "I shan't do it ," replied the fair one; "I'll throw them where I please." Young was silent for a time, but became so annoyed that he again said, "Amelia, I wish you would'nt do that any more." "I don't care," replied the spouse pettishly, "I'll throw the shells where I please, and I'll do as I please, and you may help yourself." And pulling her guest by the dress, she said; "Come, let's go up stairs and let him grunt it out."

The theatre was dedicated by prayer and a grand ball. This was in the winter of 1862-63. Brigham led off in the dance with Amelia, and all was smiles and sunshine. On another occasion, he honored another one of the women with his hand for the first cotillion. This so displeased Amelia, that she refused to dance with him at all. He coaxed, she shrugged her shoulders, and shook her head. It was only after much condescension and solicitation on his part, that she so far granted him forgiveness as to consent to dance with him. This gay Lothario of sixty-three then led forth his blushing mistress, and "all went merry as a marriage bell."

Amelia has lovers still, for one of whom she entertains considerable feeling. He was sent to "Dixie," the cotton country, in Southern Utah, on a mission. He soon returned, however, to Salt Lake City, and caused Brigham a good deal of anxiety.

Amelia is tyrannical, and rules the women of the Harem with a strong hand. They may rave, repine, or "cry their eyes out," but so long as Amelia is Queen of Brigham's heart, it will do no good.

Mrs. Emeline Free Young has been very melancholy since Brigham married Amelia.

When the Prophet "took" Amelia, poor Emeline was heart-broken. She was taken very sick and her life was, for a long time despaired of.

From her "sisters" she received no sympathy. The bitter cup which they had been obliged to drink, was now commended to her own lips.

From the confiding and happy wife, she has become the rejected and suffering mistress, and must now drag out the remainder of her days, a faded, cast off woman. And Amelia, what of her? She too, will soon take her place by the side of Emeline, and other and younger women take the place she now occupies, and in their order be cast off, to suffer with her.

"In fact," said my friend "all the women are

miserable and unhappy. It is a common remark in reply to the usual salutation, "Oh, I've got the blues to-day."

Will not Amelia soon begin to lose her influence over the Prophet and he be seeking "other worlds to conquer," I said to my friend?

She laughingly said,—"Oh, then you hav'nt heard the latest news. Brother Brigham is paying very particular attention to a charming lady whom you know.—Miss Selima Ursenbach."

How does the haughty Amelia like that?

"Oh, she is very much depressed, but she is so proud and unfeeling that nobody is sorry for her. Would you like to hear Miss Ursenbach's history?" Most assuredly, I replied, and she went on: "Miss Selima Ursenbach is a native of Geneva, Switzerland, and with her parents and brother came to Utah in the fall of 1862. She is an accomplished musician, and at once became a favorite with the Mormons. Several concerts were given, at which she figured as *prima donna*, and although she sang in French, the melody of her voice and the artistic character of her music gained for her an established reputation.

Brigham heard and was delighted. Her voice was music to his ravished ear, and for the thirtieth time, the little god let slip his arrow, and launched it into the Prophet's heart.

Says a celebrated writer:

"Now there are various ways of getting in love. A man falls in love just as he falls down stairs. It is an accident. But when he runs in love, it is as when he runs in debt: it is done knowingly, intentionally and very often rashly and foolishly, even if not ridiculously, miserably and ruinously.

"The rarest and happiest marriages are between those who have grown in love. Take the description of such a love in its rise and progress, ye thousands and tens of thousands who have what is called a taste for poetry. Take it in the sweet words of one of the sweetest and tenderest of English poets, and then say whether this is not the way that leads to happiness and bliss.

" 'Ah! I remember well [and how can I
But evermore remember well] when first
Our flame began; when scarce we knew what was
The flame we felt. When as we sat and sighed,
And looked upon each other, and conceived
Not what we ailed,—yet something we did ail;
And yet were well, and yet we were not well;
And what was our disease, we could not tell.
Then would we kiss, then sign, then look; and thus,
In that first garden ef our simpleness,
We spent our childhood. But when years began
To reap the fruit of knowledge, ah, then
Would she with graver looks, with sweet, stern brow,
Check my presumption, and my forwardness;
Yet still would give me flowers, still would me show
What she would have me, yet not have me know.' "

Is it possible I said that a man past 60, could become so infatuated with a young girl as Brigham is said to have been with Selima?

"Oh, yes," replied my friend "it has been the

talk of the church for several months. Many of the more sensible have severely censured Brother Brigham."

The same author, whose beautiful lines you quote, has somewhere said that,—

"Falling in love, and running in love, are, as everybody knows, common enough, and yet less so than what I shall call catching love. Where the love itself is imprudent, that is to say, where there is some just, prudential cause or impediment why the two parties should not be joined together in holy matrimony, there is culpable imprudence in catching it, because danger is always to be apprehended, which may have been avoided."

My friend smiling said, "your quotation is apt, for it is plain to be seen, our Prophet did not walk into love—he did not run into it. He caught it, as a man catches the measles. It broke out and showed itself all over, in smiles, bows and sweet, honeyed tones. It is also plain that he should not have caught it. Had he not the charming Amelia, dear Emeline, sweet Lucy, pretty Twiss, his darling Lucy No. 2, meek Zina, poetic Eliza, and his dear, dear Jemima, Martha, Ellen, Susan, Hattie, etc., etc. How could any man, much less a prophet, wish for more?

But he said to himself, "I have not a French lady in the family to teach my daughters that charming language. I have no *prima donna* to conduct their musical education. Then my last

love—my pretty, naughty bewitching Amelia—
is so cross and fretful, she leads me such a crazy
life, she frets and scolds, and I cannot drown her
voice, even with my 'sacred fiddle." [He has
frequently boasted that with his violin he could
put a stop to the scolding of any of his women.]

"Then my French lady is accomplished. She
can receive my foreign guests. She is so clever
that she can assist me in my business projects
and plans; and if she should prove unkind—
which God grant she may not—I should have a
great advantage—*I could not understand her.*
Then her name—Selima! How poetical. None
of my wives have such a poetical name. With
her in my Harem, I could rival the Sultan himself. Yes, sweet adored Selima, you shall be
mine. You shall be the high priestess of my
affections, and all my common women shall serve
you."

The Prophet plead his suit, but Selima was
like stone. He had a young man in his employ
who dared to love Selima. The rival lovers met
face to face. The Prophet was furious. "She is
not for you, sir, she is not for you. Leave my
service, and never dare to aspire to that young
lady's hand again."

Alas, that love so devoted, so pure and disin-
terested as Brigham's, should fail to be rewarded

by the object of its choice. But no sooner had the poor singing master, for such he was, left the Territory for California, than another rival appeared in the field—a California volunteer—a dangerous rival; one who would not fear to follow up any advantage he might gain over his spiritual competitor.

To destroy the romance of the whole story, Selima, charming but sensible Selima, becoming disgusted with the whole affair, soon after left for Switzerland again, leaving her lovers to settle the matter among themselves.

CHAPTER XXI.

THE SECRET ORDERS.

From Mr. Burlingame's Journal.

We were sitting around a cheerful open fire a few evenings ago, when we heard a hesitating step on the front porch and afterwards a faint rap at the door. I arose and opened the door and a man, rather poorly clad, and apparently in great distress, entered. I told him to be seated and to feel that he was safe, among friends.

This seemed to reassure him, and as he became more comfortable he seemed inclined to talk.

Mrs. Burlingame brought in coffee and refreshments, for we had many times before sheltered and fed those who were fleeing from Brigham's wrath. This man was an "apostate."

He believed Brigham to be a false Prophet and had embraced the doctrines of Joseph Morris whom he held to be the "True Prophet of the Lord."

I asked him if this was the first "apostasy" from Brigham since the founding of that Church.

He replied that there had been one other known as the "Gladdenites." "How did the Church authorities get rid of them?" I asked.

"In the usual way, by persecution and death."

"This first apostasy," he continued, "was headed by Gladden Bishop in 1852–53, and his followers were called Gladdenites. If you want to see how they were handled I will show you a sermon preached by Brigham Young." With this he produced from an old pocket-book a piece of newspaper yellow with age. The following extracts will show the animus of the whole:

"I will ask, What has produced your persecutions and sorrow? What has been the starting-point of all your afflictions? They began with apostates in your midst; those disaffected spirits caused others to come in, worse than they, who would run out and bring in all the devils they possibly could. That has been the starting-point and grand cause of all our difficulties, every time we were driven. I am coming to this place,—I am coming nearer home.

. . . "Do we see apostates among us now? We do.

"When a man comes right out like an independent devil, and says, 'Damn Mormonism and all the Mormons,' and is off with himself to California, I say he is a gentleman by the side of a nasty, sneaking apostate, who is opposed to nothing but Christianity. I say to the former, 'Go in peace, sir, and prosper if you can.' But we have a set of spirits here, worse than such a character. When I went from meeting last Sabbath, my ears were saluted with an apostate, crying in the streets here. I want to know if any one of you who has got the spirit of Mormonism in you would say 'Let us hear both sides of the question. Let us listen and prove all things.' What do you want to prove? Do you want to prove that an old apostate, who has been cut off from the church thirteen times for lying, is anything worthy of notice? I heard that a certain picture-dealer in this city, when the boys would have moved away the wagon in which this apostate was standing, became violent with them, saying, 'Let this man alone; these are saints that you are persecuting.' [Sneeringly.]

"We want such men to go to California, or any where they choose. I say to those persons, You must not court persecution here, lest you get so much of it you will not know what to do with it. Do NOT court persecution. We have known Gladden Bishop for more than twenty years, and know him to be a poor dirty curse. Here is sister Vilate Kimball, brother Heber's wife, has borne more from that man than any other woman on earth could bear; but she won't bear it again. I say again, you Gladdenites, do not court persecution, or you will get more than you want, and it will come quicker than you want it.

"I say to you, Bishops, do not allow them to preach in your wards. Who broke the roads to these valleys? Did this little nasty Smith, and his wife? No. They stayed in

St. Louis while we did it, peddling ribbons, and kissing the gentiles. I know what they have done here,—they have asked exorbitant prices for their nasty, stinking ribbons. [Voices, 'That's true.'] We broke the roads to this country.

"Now, you Gladdenites, keep your tongues still, lest sudden destruction come upon you. I say, rather than that a. postates should flourish here, I will unsheath my bowie knife, and conquer or die. [Great commotion in the congregation, and a simultaneous burst of feeling, assenting to the declaration.] Now, you nasty apostates, clear out, or 'judgment will be laid to the line, and righteousness to the plummet.' [Voices generally, 'Go it, go it.'] If you say it is all right, raise your hands. [All hands up.] Let us call upon the Lord to assist us in this and every other good work."

In the same discourse he commanded the Bishops to "kick these men out of their wards," and warned the apostates themselves that "they were not playing with shadows," but it was the voice and hand of the Almighty they were trying to play with, and they would find themselves mistaken if they thought to the contrary."

In accordance with this bloody teaching, many unfortunate apostates who were unwilling or unable to leave the country, "bit the dust." They felt the literal edge of the bowie-knife thus from the pulpit unsheathed for their destruction.

Many of the murders committed during the succeeding six or seven years were fully authorized by these instructions; and yet Brigham, unable to deny that they had been committed, has openly boasted that his enemies have been unable to trace any of them to him, and fasten them upon him.

He unsheathes the bowie-knife, and issues a general mandate, but when the murder of some individual dissenter is brought to his door, he turns away and says, "Thou canst not say I did it."

The second organized opposition to Young was made by Joseph Morris.

On the 19th of November, 1860, a man dressed in ordinary working-clothes wended his way on foot from Slaterville, a settlement in Weber County, north of Salt Lake, to the Holy City.

This was Joseph Morris, and the object of his visit was to deliver to Brigham Young two letters which he had written, under the influence of the Spirit.

It seems that for some reason the life of Morris had been threatened, and having been driven from the place where he had been living, he was now going to appeal to the President in person for protection. Morris had received, previous to this time, many revelations, some of which looked to a purification of the church,—all of which he had communicated to Brigham and the Apostles.

On his way to Salt Lake he met John Cook, brother of Richard Cook, at that time a Mormon

Bishop, presiding at South Weber. To him Morris communicated his views and projects, and made so favorable an impression that both the Cooks soon afterward espoused his cause, and became his zealous supporters.

Morris delivered his letters to the President at his residence, but received no reply.

He then proceeded to the house of Mr. Cook on Weber River, about thirty miles northward from the city.

Not only the Cooks, but a number of their neighbors, now began to entertain favorable opinions of the claim of their new acquaintance to inspiration.

Others who conceived that the divine right of Brigham was being endangered or infringed upon, determined to put Morris to death, or drive him from their midst. But Bishop Cook stood in the way.

In this emergency President Young was appealed to, who sent two high ecclesiastics, Messrs. John Taylor and Willford Woodruff, both Apostles, to investigate the matter. They appointed a general meeting at South Weber, and invited the Bishops of the surrounding settlements, with as many of their people as possibly could, to attend.

The meeting convened on the 11th of February, 1861, and the delegates commenced their court of inquiry by demanding whether there was a man in the ward who professed to be a prophet? And whether there were any individuals who entertained him, or professed faith in his claims?

To the astonishment and consternation of the Mormons, seventeen of the believers, with Bishop Cook at their head, arose and declared that they would enjoy and defend the right of conscience by adhering to their new faith, though it should bring upon them the most bitter persecution, and the loss of their lives. An old man named Watts arose, and in an inflammatory speech, recommended that the adherents of the new Prophet should be 'cut off under the chin,' and laid away in the brush; at the same time accompanying his words with a motion of the hand, drawing it accross his throat. This, he said, was what ought to be done, according to his understanding of the laws of the church.

After some further discussion, in which Watts was boldly rebuked by Cook for the utterance of such sentiments, the question was put to the parties on trial, whether they believed that Brigham Young was a Prophet, Seer, and Revelator.

They all answered in the negative. Mr. Taylor testified that he knew Brigham to be such and said those who believed to the contrary must be excommunicated from the church.

They were then subjected to the process of excommunication.

It will be noticed that the right of Brigham to preside over the church as its temporal head, was not questioned by Morris or his followers.

From this time the followers of Morris increased in numbers with wonderful rapidity.

On the 6th of April, 1861, five persons were baptized into the new church in the Weber River.

On the same day of the same month, thirty-one years previous, the Mormon Church had been instituted by the baptism of six persons.

Encouraged by this augury, a church was organized and the work commenced in earnest.

Converts flocked to them from all parts of the Territory.

In three months the new church numbered about five hundred.

In the meantime difficulties arose between them and the surrounding Mormons. The Morrisites refused to train as militia. Heavy fines were imposed in consequence, and much property sold on execution for their payment.

These fines and exactions were increased until the Morrisites refused longer to submit to them.

A number of fines of $60 each had been im-

APOSTASY AND FLOUR. 241

posed. When the sheriff appeared and proposed to arrest those who would not or could not pay, he was resisted. Further proceedings were then suspended for the present.

In the spring of 1862 a team, consisting of two yoke of cattle, which had been sent to mill from the Morrisite settlement, was, together with a load of flour, seized and retained by one William Jones, who threatened in like manner to retain all that should be sent until some difficulties between him and them should be settled to his satisfaction. The Morrisites, standing in immediate need of the flour, sent a *posse* of men and took not only the flour, but Jones and two associates prisoners.

Application was now made to Chief Justice Kinney, who immediately issued writs for the arrest of the leading Morrisites, and writs of *habeas corpus* for the Mormons held in custody.

These writs being disregarded, a *posse* of several hundred men, headed by Robert T. Burton, sheriff of Salt Lake County, well armed and equipped, and having several pieces of cannon, were sent to execute the writs, and enforce obedience. This force was augmented on the way by volunteers, and additional arms, until they approached the settlement of the Morrisites, with a force of about a thousand well armed men, and five pieces of artillery.

Early on the morning of the 13th of June, some of the *posse* appeared on the heights above South Weber settlement, and took possession of the Morrisites' cow-herd, killing such as they desired for beef. During the morning, Sheriff Burton sent a proclamation to the leaders within the Morrisite "fort"—for such they had constructed,—calling upon them to come out and deliver themselves up, according to the requirements of the writs in his hands, and warning them of the consequences, if they refused.

This not being responded to, about an hour later the *posse*, most of whom had been hitherto out of sight, commenced to defile over the bluffs, and to occupy a prominent position commanding the camp.

Morris now called a meeting of those within the fort. Scarcely had they assembled, when a cannon-ball came into the congregation, killed two women, and wounded a girl. From this time cannonading and musketry fire was continued with but little intermission.

The camp consisted of a few houses built of willows like basket-work, and plastered, and of tents, and covered wagons. Still the fight was kept up by these poor people for three days, during all which time, fighting with the energy of desperation, they held this immense force at bay. On the evening of the third day a white flag was raised, and the whole camp surrendered.

The Morrisites stacked their arms, under guard of a detail from the *posse*, who had by this time entered the fort.

Amidst much confusion, the men and women were separated, and large numbers of the men were placed under arrest. Morris and Banks were shot in cold blood; also two of the women.

After the Morrisites had been taken prisoners their houses were searched and plundered, and property, consisting of watches, jewelry, clothing &c., taken, to the amount of many hundreds of dollars. The prisoners were taken to Salt Lake City, and placed under bonds by Judge Kinney for their appearance at his court. They were afterwards tried, and large numbers of them were fined and imprisoned.

"Did you say" I asked, "that Morris was killed after the Morrisites had surrenderd?" "Yes," he replied, "the white flag was flying, the people had given up their arms, which were guarded by a large *posse* of Mormons.

"Robert T. Burton and Judson L. Stoddard rode in amongst the Morrisites. Burton was much excited. He said, 'Where is the man? I don't know him.' Stoddard replied, 'That's him,' pointing to Morris. Burton rode his horse upon Morris, and commanded him to give himself up in the name of the Lord. Morris replied 'No, never, never.' Morris said he wanted to speak to the people. Burton said, 'Be d—d quick about it.' Morris said, 'Brethren, I've taught you true principles,'—he had scarcely got the words out of his mouth before Burton fired his revolver. The ball passed in his neck or shoulder. Burton exclaimed, 'There's your Prophet.' He fired again, saying, 'What do you think of your Prophet now?'

"Burton then turned suddenly and shot Banks who was standing five or six paces distant. Banks fell. Mrs. Bowman, wife of James Bowman, came running up, crying, 'Oh! you bloodthirsty wretch.' Burton said, 'No one shall tell me that and live,' and shot her dead. A Danish woman then came running up to Morris, crying, and Burton shot her dead also. Burton could easily have taken Morris and Banks prisoners, if he had tried.

"I am here to-night to ask your assistance in obtaining a pardon for my unfortunate brethren.

"We have lost everything we possessed, and Brigham has forbidden any good Mormon to give us food, shelter or work, and has commanded the Danites to do their duty, which means to kill on sight any one of us who may be caught away from witnesses of the crime." "Well, my friend," said I, "whatever I can do for your people will be cheerfully done and I have no doubt at all that Gov. Harding will pardon all who are still in prison. Moreover I think we can do something for your people to get them away from the clutches of the despot. I will talk with the governor and Gen. Connor about it and let you know. His countenance brightened and he expressed his gratitude in the most unbounded terms. Finding him to be a very intelligent man I asked him, under what law or authority these outrages were committed."

He hesitated, but finally said, "I have sworn on pain of the most horrid death, never to reveal the "secrets of Mormonism" but my life is forfeited to the church any way, and a bad oath is better broken than kept and you ought to know the machinery of the most cruel despotism on the face of the earth, in order to be able to overthrow it. These horrid crimes are all done by the order and under the authority of the SECRET ORDERS OF THE CHURCH."

"It seems to me," I said, "this is a little better than an absolute despotism, where the lives and property of the people are entirely under the control and at the disposal of *one man.*"

"Yes he replied, this is a Theocratic monarchy and the President of the Church, as God's vicegerent wields despotic power over the people, and rules them by his single will, in all their affairs, both spiritual and temporal. In order that the most perfect discipline should be enforced, there is an organized system, so complete and far-reaching that the daily lives of each and every member are ready at a moment's notice to present to the President, for his inspection." I would like very much my friend to have you give me the organization of this Theocracy. He continued "you will observe as I proceed a striking similarity to the Jewish religion after which the whole system is modeled.

"Indeed we all believe that we are the chosen people of God and that we are commanded to fulfil the prophecy and are "To establish Zion on the tops of these mountains" and that all nations will flow unto it. The Morrisites hold that Brigham Young is a false and wicked king like unto Saul and that he has corrupted the faith delivered to the Saints, added thereto base and hellish practices and that God will in his own good time overthrow him and all his willing dupes and raise up a true successor to Joseph who shall re-establish his church in its purity and power.

The organization of the Mormon system is:

First,—THE FIRST PRESIDENCY. This consists of three, chosen from those who hold the high-priesthood and apostleship, and its office is to preside over and direct the affairs of the whole church. The President is also Seer, Revelator, Translator, and Prophet. He rules in all spiritual and temporal affairs.

Secondly,—THE APOSTLES. These are to build up, organize, and preside over churches, administer the ordinances, etc.

Thirdly,—THE SEVENTIES. The Quorums of the Seventies are to travel in all the world, preach the gospel, and administer its ordinances and blessings. There is, also, the Patriarch, whose duty it is to bless the fatherless, to prophesy what shall befall them, etc.

Fourthly,—HIGH-PRIESTS AND ELDERS. The High-Priest is to administer the ordinances, and preside over the *Stakes* of the church; that is, over the churches established abroad.

The Elders are to preach and to baptize; to ordain other Elders, also Priests, Teachers, and Deacons. All the foregoing officers are of the Milchisedec Priesthood.

Fifthly,—THE AARONIC PRIESTHOOD, which includes the offices of Bishop, Priest, Teacher, and Deacon.

The Bishop presides over all the lesser offices of the Aaronic Priesthood, ministers in outward ordinances, conducts the temporal business of the church, and sits in judgment on transgressors.

The Priest is to preach, baptize, administer the sacrament of the Lord's Supper, and visit and exhort the saints.

The Teacher is to watch over and strengthen the church, etc.

The Deacon is to assist the Teacher.

There is also a High Council, consisting of Twelve High-Priests, with a President. The office of the Council is to settle all important difficulties.

The Priesthood comes direct from Heaven, and was lost to man, until the keys of both orders of the Priesthood were given to Joseph Smith, by an angel from Heaven, in 1829.

After the death of Smith, they came into the hands of Brigham Young.

From this *resume* of the church organization, it will be seen that it is sufficient for the purpose. Nor is it confined to spiritual affairs.

Under the form of a church organization, this system absorbs not only the religious, but all the civil and political liberty of the individual member. The High Council forms an apparent check on the power of the President; but when it is considered that this body is composed of persons nearest the President, and under his immediate influence and control, in other relations in the same organization,—as High-Priests, etc.,—it will be seen that the check is only nominal.

The orders of the Priesthood, to which these officers are respectively attached, are thus distinguished:—

The Melchisedec Priesthood hold the right of Presidency, receive revelations from Heaven, for the guidance of the church, and hold the keys of all its spiritual blessings.

The Aaronic Priesthood hold the keys of the ministering of angels, and have the right to administer in outward ordinances. This Priesthood must be filled by lineal descendants of Aaron.

It will be seen that the mission of all the officers of the Melchisedec Priesthood, the Apostles, High-Priests, Seventies, and Elders—is to propagate the gospel, and make converts; while the government of the church and of the people is committed to the Aaronic Priesthood.

Of these the chief is the Bishop, who is accordingly the civil and religious magistrate of the ward in which he resides.

The Order of the Danites has been, for many years, an established institution in the Mormon church.

It was first organized as the Daughters of Zion, see Songs of Solomon and Isaiah 4.4. Then on July 4th, 1838, as the Danite Band or United Brothers of Gideon, with the battle cry of "The Sword of the Lord and Gideon," see Judges, chapters 6, 7, 8. Also Genesis 46. 17. "Dan shall be a serpent by the way, an adder in the path, that biteth the horses' heels, so that his rider shall fall backward."

Brigham Young and his two Counselors form the First Presidency, under the title of the Gods, or Grand Archees. These are, at present, Young, Kimball, and Wells. A few, also, of the Apostles, hold the rank of Grand Archees. These have the power of life and death.

Next in importance, is a body of men called Archees. They are entitled to sit in Council with the Gods or Grand Archees, in matters relating to the taking of life. This "Quorum" as it is called, also includes some of the Bishops and Presidents of other quorums in in the church.

Their office is to examine cases of offenders thought to require a summary disposal, and submit the result of such examination to the Grand Archees. In some cases, where the utmost discretion is required, they act as agents and swift-winged messengers, to carry into effect the decrees of the Gods.

The Archees have discretionary and independent power over the lives of all gentiles and "apostates."

Next in rank are the Danites, whose office is to assist the Archees in the execution of their bloody deeds. These are formed into bands of fifty men each. One band, at least, belongs to each Archee, they serving under him as minute men. These "Danite Bands" are generally composed of inferior officers and teachers, constables, and policemen, and those who, having committed heinous crimes, as murder, theft, adultery, &c., would sooner be sworn to serve in this bloody office, than have their deeds exposed and receive their justly merited punishment.

The officers in all these grades are solemnly sworn to secrecy, and to the duties of their respective offices, on pain of instant death.

Where the danger of discovery is imminent, and the matter in hand is too important to be trusted to the Danites, the Archees meet and perform the dirty work themselves; as in the case of Secretary Babbitt, Brewer, and the unlucky attempt on Dr. Hurt. In other cases, the Danites are called upon; instance the Parishes, Potter,

Bowman, Mountain Meadows, &c.

The Danites are expected to act as spies upon the federal officers and other gentiles; to watch the feelings and spirits of the saints, and to report the first indications of disaffection.

Such cases are at once attended to, and if they are deemed of a dangerous character, are summarily disposed of.

The spoil is divided, one half going to the Grand Archees, and the other half to the Archees and Danites who are employed in the commission of the crime.

When Judge Cradlebaugh attempted to bring to justice the perpetrators of the Mountain Meadow Massacre, and various other crimes, several bishops and many other leading Mormons fled to the mountains, where they remained several weeks. Their place of refuge they named "Mount Kolob," which means "the residence of the Gods."

The remark is frequently made in Utah,— "Brigham is the only God I care a d—n about."

The deep meaning of this is only to be explained by reference to this organized system of crime taken in connection with the organization of the "celestial kingdom."

The theory is that Brigham Young is a God in embryo. That he is laying the foundation here for a celestial kingdom. That there will be created for him a world, which his posterity will inhabit, and of which he will be the King and God.

His kingdom will be constituted as follows:

1st. Himself as God.

2d. His wives as Goddesses and Queens, each ruling her own posterity, with Brigham as husband and God.

3d. His sons and their families.

4th. The daughters by the celestial law would when married, pass out of their father's kingdom and be added to the husband's. To obviate this difficulty, every man who marries one of the President's daughters is obliged to be adopted by and sealed to his father-in-law.

The daughter is thus retained to augment her father's kingdom, by the addition of her family.

This is one reason why female children are so lightly esteemed in Utah. They cannot add to the father's glory, but must go to glorify others.

5th. Many young men who have no families and therefore no kingdoms, are sealed to Brigham, to add to his celestial glory,—in some instances, also, men of families, who have not ambition enough to aspire to kingdoms of their own.

This relationship pertains to this world as well as to the next. Brigham becomes a father to them here, supports them if necessary, and demands their respect and obedience.

A case recently occurred in Salt Lake, which fully illustrates the power which Young exercises over this class of his subjects.

Dr. Sprague, an eastern man, has been at Salt Lake about twelve years. During most of that time he has officiated in the Endowment House, in the washings and anointings. He has also had charge of the Tabernacle, and acted as family physician to the inmates of the Harem.

He has a wife and two children. His son is on a mission, and the daughter, a little girl of thirteen, is an invalid. Mrs. Sprague is a model New-England housewife. She has toiled early and late to procure the comforts, and some of the luxuries of life. By the most persevering effort, they at length succeeded in building a beautiful house, and Doctor Sprague's garden is the prettiest in Salt Lake.

The family removed to their new residence in the fall of 1862, and had but just furnished it.

By the Mormon law of adoption, the property of the adopted child belongs to the father, or is under his control. Dr. Sprague is the adopted son of Brigham Young. His whole property is worth not less than $10,000.

Mrs. Emeline Free Young has been very melancholy since Brigham married Amelia. Her health continued to decline until it was thought advisable to remove her from the Lion House the scene of her joys and sorrow, and situate her more pleasantly. Accordingly one day Brigham called on Dr. Sprague and wife, and coolly told them that he wanted their place for three or four years, for Emeline, until he could build her one. At the end of that time they could have it again, and in the meantime they could live in the house formerly occupied by J. M. Grant, which he would have repaired for their use.

The husband and wife were astonished and confounded at this request, and Mrs. Sprague, under the first impulse of her indignation, said "she did not relish the idea of giving up her house to people who read novels every day." "Very well," replied the Prophet, "if you prefer to incur my displeasure rather than to let me have your home, you can do so." With this he left them.

The Doctor and his wife began thinking the matter over. It would never do to incur the displeasure of brother Brigham. He was their father in this world, and their God in the celestial kingdom. Then the Doctor was advancing in years, and should he lose his situation in the Endowment House and Tabernacle, where would be the support for himself and family in his declining years? He had served his adopted father so long and faithfully, should he break with him now? It would never do; so, after many sleepless nights and much anguish of spirit, he made up his mind to make the sacrifice. As to Mrs. Sprague, she cared not for herself, but her poor sick child! She had lived for years almost entirely in the beautiful garden, and how could she leave it now? With frail and faltering step she had wandered amid the flowers and fruit, culling this bright geranium and that lovely rose, plucking this beautiful strawberry, and that luscious bunch of grapes, and by this sweet communion with Nature, the child seemed to receive afresh the life-giving principle. She was now to be torn from her little paradise, by whom and for what? No wonder if the heart of the mother grew somewhat stony at the reflection.

When the poor girl heard that she must leave these "delightful shades," she wept until oblivion wrapt her senses, and in a fit of convulsions, she forgot, for the time being, at least, her cruel fate.

The sisters came to sympathize with Sister Sprague; said it was too bad. "Sister Sprague, it is too bad, but you had better do it than to have Brother Brigham's curse resting upon you."

Emeline, who is really very kind-hearted, came and wept with Sister S., saying she did not want her home, "but Brigham," said she, "has set his mind upon it, and we don't any of us *dare* to speak to him about it."

Young remained inexorable—the change was made; and to-day the whilome favored wife and now cast-off mistress of Brigham Young, occupies the beautiful residence of Dr. Sprague, the fruit of his many years of toil and economy.

It is an ordinary thing for people who offend in any way the Archees to be got out of the way.

The order is given to "cut them off just under the chin." Brigham does not in words sanction this, but simply crooks his little finger and says "the boys know their business."

When John D. Lee, and his "band" had got the emigrants from Missouri and Arkansas in such a position that he knew he could cut them off if he wanted to do it he sent a courier to Brigham for further instruction. Mrs. Emeline Free happened to be near when the messenger arrived and found out his business and got down on her knees and begged for the lives of these emigrants, but she could not move the heart of this cruel king; but like the despot of old he ordered the slaughter to go on, saying, "They have shed the blood of the Saints and I command you in the name of Israel's God to follow these cursed gentiles and disguised as Indians attack them and with the arrows of the

Almighty make a clean sweep of them and leave none to tell the tale." You know the result.

This was the richest train that ever crossed the plains and you can see any day among the leaders of this people the pianos, fine clothing and splendid horses and carriages which were taken from them.

"It seems" said I, "that these people stop at no crime when they have an object to accomplish." "No," said he, "they consider that they are doing God's service just as much when committing a murder of the most horrible description as when attending divine services in the tabernacle, provided they are under the instructions of their superiors. The other day I was conversing with a man high in the Priesthood, and he said:

"Some time in the summer of 1851, I went to the Mint, in Salt Lake City, on business. John Kay was there. He had charge of the Mint. The building is now inside of Brigham's Wall. On a table, a little to one side of the room I saw a human skeleton complete, attached by wires. I asked him how it came there. After some reluctance, he stated that it was the skeleton of an emigrant, who was passing through Salt Lake, and who had boasted how he had assisted in persecuting the Mormons in Missouri. He said he would continue to persecute them, and lived for that purpose, or something like that. Kay said, 'We asked Brigham what we were to do with him.' Brigham replied, 'He supposed the boys knew their business.' I then asked Kay how they managed it. He said they invited the emigrant to the Mint, to see the works, and take a drink with them.

"Having arrived there, as he was stepping down some steps which led to the furnace, Kay struck him, as he said on the top of the head, with a wooden mallet, which knocked him senseless. He did not say how he proceeded after that. I asked him how he took the flesh from the bones.

"He said, with vitriol and lime.

"I have often heard the doctrine of cutting the throats of apostates preached from the pulpit, particularly during the year 1856, when, for several months, I scarcely attended meeting without hearing such preaching. They would say If you find a man with his throat cut, pay no attention to it.

"At one time, my life was threatened by a Danite, and his intention to take my life was sanctioned at a meeting, by the Bishop and authorities. No cause was alleged, except a trivial remark made by my wife, reflecting slightly on one of the First Presidents. The remark had been exaggerated and attributed to me, and although it was fully explained, I was followed and threatened for over a year.

"At that time my wife and myself were members of the Mormon Church, in good standing."

I have heard a great deal about the Danite leaders, have met several of them, and I must say they do not look like bad men. Bill Hickman came in one evening sat down and took my little children on his knees and talked to them in a kindly and gentle way that greatly surprised me.

I shuddered to see this hero of a dozen murders sitting familiarly at my fireside. What can be said of a religion that will turn a naturally good man into a fiend of hell?

Bill Hickman is one of the most notorious of the Danite leaders. He is a man of medium size, heavy set, of florid complexion, troubled of late years with weak eyes, causing him to wear goggles. He is now about fifty years of age. He is of Southern birth, and a strong secessionist, but professes much friendship for the United States Government, and for federal officers. He is wily and cunning, with much of the *suaviter in modo*, and is something of a lawyer. He glories in a household of seven "women" and about twenty children, but does not maintain them in the highest style.

Porter Rockwell, another noted character, is somewhat of the same style of Hickman. Shorter of stature, with the Utah floridity of complexion, and very voluble in conversation. Anything that is all right with Rockwell, is "on the square." It is "wheat," and nearly every act and expression of a stranger, is of that character.

Robert T. Burton, Sheriff of Salt Lake County, and Collector of Internal Revenue, who bids fair to rival or outdo all the others in his lawless deeds is a tall, wiry man, one it would be hard to hit with a bullet. He is cool and imperturbable; in fact, never thrown off his balance, never wanting in case of an emergency. No fitter person to carry out the plans of Young could be found within or without the Territory, and upon him Brigham relies implicitly. With or without a "writ," he is always ready.

The history of the rise and progress of the religion of Mahomet, as well as of most of the religions of the past, furnishes us with abundant instances of the crimes which fanatical zeal, inspired by what is supposed to be divine revelation, will lead men to commit. The enemies of the Lord and His annointed are to them no more than the "adder in the path," and they would cut them off with as much zeal as they would perform any other religious rite. The blood of their prophet cries from the ground for vengeance on his murderers, and these bold defenders of the faith will stick at no crime until they have destroyed and laid waste the land, and the people that have so cruelly wronged them. This feeling was at the bottom of the Mountain Meadow massacre, than which, there is no crime more fiendish, more dreadful and more treacherous in all history.

CHAPTER XXII.

SOCIETY IN THE SIERRAS.

From Mrs. Burlingame's Journal.

I have been so absorbed in the affairs around me, so much interested in the religion, customs and doings of "this peculiar people," that I have almost forgotten my friends who crossed the plains with us.

Miss Julia has written me a long letter from her home in the Sierras, which I will write down here that it may be in a form for convenient reference.

SIERRA SEMINARY, JAN. 15th, 1863.

My Dear Sister,

When I arrived here I found Aunt Kizzie, waiting to receive me with open arms. She is one of the dearest and best of women. She is just the kind of a go-a-head woman you would like. She is Principal of Sierra Seminary, a large and flourishing school for young ladies and a heavy dealer in Mining Stocks. Gov. Nye says that Miss Clapp is one of the shrewdest operators in stocks he ever knew. Her Seminary is the center of the social world and in her beautiful and elegant apartments are frequently gathered the great men of this region.

Here politics, literature, science and religion are freely discussed and no one is tabooed on account of his opinions.

I must give you some account of our holiday festivities. On Christmas eve we held our closing reception. The examinations were over and the evening was devoted to music, dancing and social entertainment. Many of our patrons were here and I assure you they were well pleased with the manner in which their daughters had been trained. We had some very unique characters present, Gov. Nye, Senator Johns, General Jordan, Col. Pray, Judge Beattie, Capt. Mounts, Col. Sellers and several members of the legislature. There are no plain citizens here. All wear titles, with as much ease and nonchalance as they wear their watch guards. Several of the gentlemen considered it their duty to play the agreeable to your humble servant. Gen. Jordan, a bonanza king was exceedingly gracious and told me rather in confidence that his mines were the richest in the world but that he thought best to be a little quiet about it for the present.

He said that his wife should blaze with diamonds and have the finest "outfit" in all Paris.

This was rather suggestive for a single man of 50 and I felt a little blush creeping up into my cheek. As soon as possible I turned the conversation and addressed myself to Capt. Mounts who is quite a character here. He has made his "pile" in mining phrase and instead of branching out he is looking about him with great caution. I said, Capt. I suppose you will be buying into some of the bonanzas soon? "No" said he, "I shall not go into anything new unless it is a *"dead thing,"* in fact said he "it must be VERY DEAD." I think I will go down to the land of big apples and pretty girls, get me a wife and settle down." Sensible Captain!

Senator Johns and Judge Beattie were discussing the political situation and as they were on different sides and both candidates for the U. S. Senate their language at times became more forcible than elegant, though I must give western men the credit of showing a hearty appreciation of, and genuine respect for the sex.

These men are wholesouled, brave, generous to a fault and though not quite so refined in

NEW YEAR CALLERS. 265

manner are more truly noble and polite than their eastern brethren.

After the exercises an elegant collation was served. Music and dancing, games and cards, and social intercourse, according to the taste of the guest, made the evening a very delightful one and long to be remembered by those who participated in this pleasant reunion.

I must tell you of our New Year callers.

Miss Clapp is a great favorite here and as every body feels at liberty to make calls on his lady friends on the first day of the year we had a decided variety I do assure you.

Our first caller was Capt. Brown. He was one of those long, lean, cadaverous yankees with a great many peculiarities. "A happy new year Capt." said Miss Clapp, "how are your mines doing?" "I think" said the Capt. "that we shall soon strike it rich and I shall go down east with a pocket full of rocks!"

The Capt. represents a large class who are always just going to strike "pay rock" but never do.

Col. Sellers next arrived. He was gorgeous in black dress suit, white vest and lavender kids.

"Good morning ladies" said the Col. "and many happy reurns. I am so burdened with business, have so many men coming to see me about my mines that I had to transcend the laws of etiquette and make a morning call." I asked the Col. where his mines were located. "Well said he they are in the Sky-Light district, a new bonanza my dear lady, a great thing, the greatest discovery of the age; in fact "there are millions in them." "Have you struck a true fissure vein," said Miss Clapp, and what is its width?" "Well" said the Col. "we have indications which are unmistakable and our men are very sanguine that we are about to open the champion mine of the world." The Col. is at present stopping at the boarding-house of a lady to whom he has sold mining shares in "The Sky-Light" at a hundred cents on the dollar.

There is a large class of such adventurers who live by their wits and by imposing on the good nature and credulity of honest but simple hearted people.

Our next caller was "Dunbar." He came in slyly and with considerable embarrassment and after a few words of salutation drew out from under his big coat, a red bandanna, full of choice red apples which he begged to have us take saying "I reckon there aint nuthin' no better'n these ere apples this side the States." We thanked him kindly and made him as much at home as the Governors, Judges, Colonels, Captains and Brigadier Generals who thronged our parlors, from early morning until late at night. Towards night we received a call from Col. Danford, Superintendent of The Consolidated Bonanza Mines, at Virginia City. He is a model gentleman, a thorough man of the world and splendid business manager. He invited us to visit his mines and we have accepted; so I will keep this letter open until our return in order to give you an account of our journey.

Thursday, Jan. 21st. 1863.

Oh what a splendid time we have had! I had no idea of the beauty and grandeur of mountain scenery until I came on this trip. We have climbed higher, higher and at last reached the Queen City of this wonderful region. As we slowly wound our way up the mountains, long lines of teams came down loaded with the precious ore from which millions were to be extracted. Everything was bustle, life, activity.

We soon reached the famous Comstock Lode. Great piles of rock were to be seen in every direction, most of which was ready to send to the mills. When all was ready we prepared to descend the shaft of the Comstock. Down, down we went until day-light disappeared and then a faint glimmer from the "lower level lights" was visible. We were at the bottom and about 1000 ft. below the surface of the earth. A perceptible difference in temperature exists at this point and bears witness to the theory that the center of the earth is a molten mass of metals. After looking around at the rich deposits of silver rock which seemed inexhaustible, we were glad to again reach *terra firma*, and the light of day.

We had a delightful ride down the mountain, and as the stage dashed around the sharp corners of the jutting rock we could look up and see mountains rising and towering over us and looking down we could behold a yawning chasm thousands of feet deep, ready to receive us, if our trusty steeds should make a single misstep, and thus at once close our earthly career.

Here we are at home once more and long shall I remember my visit to the Comstock Lode and Virginia City. I shall probably go to San Francisco next spring. Love to you and yours,

From your Sister,

Julia Burlingame.

I was quietly sitting at home a few days ago when I was agreeably surprised to receive a call from Mr. and Mrs. Bradish on their way home to Chicago. I was glad to hear from many of our party who had gone on to California while we had remained at Salt Lake.

Mr. Patrick had gone on to the Sandwich Islands for his health, Prof. Belfield was engaged in locating and working mines in California, and Mr. Goodhue, was now editor of a leading Daily.

The Brinks were living in Sacramento, and Miss Julia, as we had before learned, had just been married to a leading lawyer in San Francisco. We had heard but little from her lately, she being, as we supposed, too busy for letter writing. Mrs. Bradish now gave us a full account of Miss Julia's stay in San Francisco.

She said "When Miss Julia arrived, she was immediately received into the choicest society in the city. Capt. and Mrs. Thome became much interested in her and insisted upon making her a member of their household. They have one of the most luxurious homes on the coast; nothing that money can buy is wanting to adorn and beautify it. Miss Julia as the young lady friend of Mrs. Thome was the admired of all admirers.

Her wit, learning, beauty and accomplishments here had full play. She conversed in several languages with the Capt.'s guests, she entertained them with piano music and accompanied her lovely voice with her "light guitar." Many admirers hovered around her. She received the attentions of all with charming naivete and condescension but gave no decided encouragement to any. Col. Preigh laid his heart and $100.000 at her feet but she kindly told him that she could not accept him but should always regard him as a good friend. Many a heart pang was endured and many offers made only to be rejected. Mining kings, millionaires with their diamonds, stocks, gold and bonds were all alike passed by and Miss Julia's heart remained her own possession. But lo, a new Richmond came on the scene. "Miss Julia," said Capt. Thome at an evening reception, "allow me to introduce to you Mr. Rudolph C. Herrington, a member of the San Francisco bar." A pleased smile lighted up her expressive features as she bowed gracefully and extended her jeweled hand. Mr. Herrington was at once struck with her beauty, grace and many accomplishments, and it was not difficult to see that the admiration was mutual.

He is a most excellent man, a fine scholar, with a keen wit and brilliant intellect. He is not rich but has what is better than money, an ability to make it. This acquaintance was not long in ripening into love and it was soon understood in society circles that the Thome Mansion was to be the scene of a brilliant wedding.

The evening came at length and society was in a flutter. Cards were out for a large reception, but the ceremony was to be performed in church.

The Rev. Dr. Wiltheron united the happy pair and then the invited guests repaired to the mansion of Capt. Thome.

A most beautiful sight greeted our eyes as we drew up before the house. Colored lights reflected from prismatic glass, threw a most bewitching charm over all surrounding objects.

The chandeliers were composed of flowers so arranged that their own natural colors were reflected by the light.

The banquet was simply superb and all enjoyed the hearty hospitality of the host. But everything must come to an end, and so the wedding over, the guests departed, one by one, leaving our hero and heroine to commence the battle of life much as all those who have gone before and as all those will who shall come after them."

CHAPTER XXIII.
From Mrs. Burlingame's Journal.
THE MISSIONARIES AND THE MORMONS.

Gen. Connor has sent a company of his men up to Soda Springs to establish a colony of the Morrisites and the Federal officers, and Gentile merchants have formed a joint stock company and have furnished these people with provisions, farming implements, seeds and everything necessary to enable them to get a start.

Mr. Burlingame has gone with the colony to look after them, lay out a town and see that their rights in the land are protected.

The day that Mr. Burlingame left Salt Lake City, he met Elder Briggs, the missionary from "The True Latter Day Saints," who have remained in Illinois, and are under the Presidency of

Joseph Smith Jr. Elder Briggs is President of the Twelve Apostles and occupies much the same position that Paul did in the early church.

Mr. Burlingame became a good deal interested, in his plan of work and as he was going away he told the Elder that he had better call and see me and I would do what I could to help him.

He is a man of great energy and heroism, and takes hold of his mighty task as though it were but the work of a summer day. Nowhere can be found a better exemplification of the self-sacrifice and sublime heroism of the Christians of the Middle Ages.

I said, "Elder Briggs I have two questions to ask you before I can promise to do anything to further your mission here. Have you come here to teach loyalty to the government of the United States, and to do everything in your power to break up polygamy?"

He replied, "The fulness of time has come," when the true church with the son of our dead Prophet at its head shall again be established and the wicked and lustful Pretender overthrown.

"I am here to uphold the laws of my country and to break up that "abomination" which Brigham and his corrupt satellites have engrafted on the church.

"I am satisfied that your mission is good and

I will do all I can do to help you. What are the doctrines of your church?" He replied, "The following are the Articles of faith of the Church of Jesus Christ of Latter Day Saints, under the Presidency of Joseph Smith, son of Joseph the Martyr:

"We believe in God, the Eternal Father, and his Son Jesus Christ, and in the Holy Ghost.

"We believe that men will be punished for their own sins and not for Adam's transgressions.

"We believe that through the atonement of Christ, all mankind may be saved by obedience to the laws and ordinances of the gospel.

"We believe that these ordinances are: 1st. Faith in the Lord Jesus Christ; 2d. Repentance; 3d. Baptism by immersion for the remission of sins; 4th. Laying on of hands for the gift of the Holy Spirit; 5th. The Lord's Supper.

"We believe that men must be called of God, by inspiration, and by laying on of hands by those who are duly commissioned to preach the gospel, and administer in the ordinances thereof.

"We believe in the same organization that existed in the primitive church, viz.: Apostles, Prophets, Pastors, Teachers, Evangelists, &c.

"We believe in the powers and gifts of the everlasting gospel, viz.: the gift of faith, discoursing of spirits, prophecy, revelation, visions, healing, tongues and the interpretation of tongues, wisdom, charity, brotherly love, &c.

"We believe the word of God recorded in the Bible; we also believe in the word of God recorded in the Book of Mormon, and in all other good books.

"We believe all that God has revealed, all that he does now reveal, and we believe that he will yet reveal many more great and important things pertaining to the kingdom God and Messiah's second coming.

"We believe in the literal gathering of Israel, and the restoration of the ten tribes; that Zion will be established upon the Western Continent; that Christ will reign personally upon the earth for a thousand years; and that the earth will be renewed, and receive its paradisaical glory.

"We believe in the literal resurrection of the body; that

the dead in Christ will rise first, and that the rest of the dead do not live again until the thousand years are expired.

"We believe in being subject to kings, queens, presidents, rulers, and magistrates; *in obeying, honoring, and sustaining the law.*

"We believe in being virtuous, chaste, temperate, benevolent, and in doing good to all men.

"*We believe the church in Utah, under the presidency of Brigham Young, have apostatized from the true order of the gospel.*

"*We believe that the doctrines of polygamy, human sacrifice, or killing men to save them, Adam being God, Utah being Zion, or the gathering place for the saints, are doctrines of devils,* instituted by wicked men, for the accomplishment of their own lustful desires, and with a view to their personal aggrandizement.

"*We believe in being true and loyal to the Government of the United States,* and have no sympathy or fellowship for the treasonable practices or wicked abominations indorsed by Brigham Young and his followers."

"It is claimed here" I said "that polygamy was established by Joseph Smith, and practised secretly and that the Revelation on the Celestial marriage was made to him." With much indignation he replied "This is but one of the false and hellish doctrines that Brigham Young has foisted upon the Church. He has arrogated to himself the title and power of God. He has promulgated the terrible doctrine of human sacrifice for the remission of sins. Jedediah M. Grant second counselor said in a sermon not long ago:

"Brethren and sisters, we want you to repent and forsake your sins. And you who have committed sins that cannot be forgiven through baptism, let your blood be shed, and let the smoke ascend, that the incense thereof may come up before God as an atonement for your sins, and that the sinners in Zion may be afraid."

Again:—

"We have been trying long enough with this people, and I go in for letting the sword of the Almighty be unsheathed, not only in word, but in deed."

In accordance with such bloody teaching, it is said that an altar of sacrifice was actually built by Grant, in the temple block, upon which these human sacrifices were to be made. On the 21st of September, 1856, Grant said;—

"I say there are men and women here that I would advise to go to the President immediately, and ask him to appoint a committee to attend to their case; and then let a place be selected, and let that committee shed their blood."

This horrible proposal to immolate upon the altar of sacrifice the erring saints, was fully endorsed by Brigham Young as follows:—

"There are sins that men commit for which they cannot receive forgiveness in this world, or in that which is to come; and if they had their eyes open to see their condition, they would be perfectly willing to have their blood spilt upon the ground, that the smoke thereof might ascend to Heaven as an offering for their sins, and the smoking incense would atone for their sins; whereas, if such is not the case, they will stick to them, and remain upon them in the spirit-world.

"I know, when you hear my brethren telling about cutting people off from the earth, that you consider it is strong doctrine. It is to save them, not to destroy them. I will say further, I have had men come to me, and offer their lives to atone for their sins. It is true that the blood of the Son of God was shed for sins, through the fall, and those committed by man, yet men can commit sins which it can never remit. As it was in ancient days, so it is in our day; and though the principles are taught publicly from this stand, still the people do not understand them; yet the Law is precisely the same. There are sins that can be atoned for by an offering upon the altar, as in ancient days, and there are sins that the blood of a lamb, of a calf, or of turtle-doves cannot remit, but they must be atoned for by the blood of the man. That is the reason why men talk to you as they do from this stand. They understand the doctrine, and throw out a few words about it."

But the greatest change of all in the Mormon religion, made by Brigham Young, was the introduction and establishment of polygamy.

This was no part of the Mormon system of religion as originally established. On the contrary it was expressly repudiated by all the Mormon writers and speakers, previous to 1852, and in Europe for some years afterward.

The Mormon religion was founded by Joseph Smith and his coadjutors, and the principles and doctrines of the religion were, in the first instance such as they established.

The Book of Mormon nowhere contains a word in favor of it. On the contrary all of its principal characters were monogamists. Such was Lehi, the patriarch of Mormon history. Such also were Ishmael and Nephi.

"Behold the Lamanites, your brethren, whom ye hate because of their filthiness and the cursings which hath come upon their skins, are more righteous than you; for they have not forgotten the commandment of the Lord, which was given unto our fathers, that they should have, save it were one wife, and concubines they should have none; and there should not be whoredoms committed among them.

"And now this commandment they observe to keep; wherefore, because of this observance, in keeping this commandment: the Lord God will not destroy them, but will be merciful unto them; and one day they shall become a blessed people."

As if to place this matter beyond any question we have the following still more explicit testimony, pages 115 and 118;—

"And now it came to pass that the people of Nephi, under the reign of the second king, began to grow hard in their hearts and indulge themselves somewhat in wicked practices such as like unto David of old, desiring many wives and concubines, and also Solomon his son.

"The word of God burdens me because of your grosser crimes. For behold, thus saith the Lord, this people begin to wax in iniquity; they understand not the Scriptures; for they seek to excuse themselves in committing whoredoms, because of the things which were written concerning David, and Solomon his son. Behold David and Solomon truly had many wives and concubines, which thing was abominable before me, saith the Lord; wherefore, thus saith the Lord, I have led this people forth out of the land of Jerusalem, by the power of mine arm, that I might raise up a righteous branch from the fruit of the loins of Joseph. Wherefore, I the Lord God, will not suffer that this people shall do like unto them of old. Wherefore, my brethren, hear me, and hearken to the word of the Lord; for there shall not any man among you have, save it be one wife; and concubines he shall have none; for I, the Lord God, delighteth in the chastity of women. And whoredoms are an abomination before me; thus saith the Lord of Hosts."

DOCTRINE AND COVENANTS.

Orson Pratt, the ablest writer on Mormon theology, is compelled to admit that the Book of Mormon is opposed to polygamy. He says;—

"Do you believe that the Book of Mormon is a divine revelation? We do. Does that book teach the doctrine of plurality of wives? It does not. Does the Lord in that book forbid the plurality doctrine? He forbid the ancient Nephites to have any more than one wife."

Let us now turn to the Book of Doctrine and Covenants, and see if we can find in that volume any authority for polygamy. The following passages will determine the question:

"Thou shalt love thy wife with all thy heart, and shalt cleave unto her, and none else; and he that looketh upon a woman to lust after her, shall deny the faith, and shall not have the spirit; and if he repents not he shall be cast out."

Again. In 1845, the year after Joseph's death an Appendix was authoritatively added to the Book of Doctrine and Covenants, containing the following, which is extracted from the section entitled "Marriage":

2. "Marriage should be celebrated with prayer and thanksgiving; and at the solemnization, the persons to be married standing together," etc., "he [the person officiating] shall say, calling each by their names, 'you both mutually agree to be each other's companion, husband and wife, observing the legal rights belonging to this condition; that is, keeping yourselves wholly for each other, and from all others, during your lives.' And when they have answered 'yes,' he shall

pronounce them 'husband and wife,' in the name of the Lord Jesus Christ, and by virtue of the laws of the country, and authority vested in him.

. . . . "Inasmuch as this church of Christ has been reproached with the crime of fornication and polygamy; we declare thst we believe that one man should have one wife; and one woman but one husband, except in case of death, when either is at liberty to marry again."

Can anything be more explicit than this? Polygamy is not only expressly repudiated by the church, but is classed by the side of fornication as a crime.

Thus we find that polygamy is contrary to both books of the Mormon Bible. That it is, in fact, strongly condemned in those volumes.

It is, therefore, no part of the Mormon religion as given to the world by Joseph Smith.

But polygamy is practised in Utah. Whence did it arise, and upon what foundation does it rest?

Like slavery, and all other great social evils, it had its origin, doubtless, in an abuse of the passions of man.

It was first publicly announced and recommended in Utah Territory on the 29th of August, 1852, by Orson Pratt and Brigham Young, at a politico-religious meeting held in Great Salt Lake City.

On that occasion, President Young said:—

"You heard Brother Pratt state, this morning, that a Revelation would be read this afternoon, which was given previous to Joseph's death. It contains a doctrine a small portion of the world is opposed to; but I can deliver a prophecy upon it. Though that doctrine was not preached by the Elders, this people have believed in it for years.

"The original copy of this Revelation was burnt up. William Clayton was the man who wrote it from the mouth of the Prophet. In the meantime it was in Bishop Whitney's possession. He wished the privilege to copy it, which Brother Joseph Smith granted. Sister Emma, [wife of Joseph Smith], burnt the original. The reason I mention this is because that the people who did know of the Revelation, suppose it was not now in existence.

"The Revelation will be read to you. The principle spoken upon by Brother Pratt this morning, we believe in.'

. . . "Many others are of the same mind. They are not ignorant of what we are doing in our social capacity. They have cried out proclaim it; but it would not do a few years ago; everything must come in its time, as there is a time to all things. I am now ready to proclaim it.

"This Revelation has been in my possession many years and who has known it? None but those who should know it. I keep a patent lock on my desk, and there does not anything leak out that should not."

"I think you have made it very plain Elder Briggs that Polygamy and all these horrid doctrines are no part of the Mormon faith, but have been introduced by a wicked, lustful and designing man to enable him to aggrandize himself and his followers at the expense of the true interests of your Church. I shall do all I can to aid you in your work for I am satisfied that a large majority of the people here are honest and would do what is right if they were not afraid of persecution."

"You have doubtless heard" said he "that Brigham has denounced Bro. Mc Cord and myself in the tabernacle and forbidden anybody to give us shelter under their roofs or to permit us to hold meetings in their houses.

"He also said he would not be responsible for our safety, which is, you know, equivalent to saying that if the Danites have a good opportunity they are commanded to "cut us off." We have no place where we can lay our heads except with a poor old man who lives in a hovel with a dirt floor and no one dare open his doors to us. If we preach in the streets we shall at once be arrested."

My indignation was thoroughly aroused, and I said, "there is one person in Salt Lake City who is not afraid of Brigham Young; you shall have my parlor to preach in and let Brigham dare to interfere."

Elder Briggs expressed his gratitude and said the Lord would bless and reward me and after arranging the preliminaries for the meeting, took his leave.

Several of the Federal Officers having heard of my determination have called to remonstrate with me for taking such risks. They said,'Your husband is away and why antagonize the mormons and bring on yourself their bitter hate?' I re-

MEETINGS OF THE JOSEPHITES. 283

plied, "Shall I stand idly by and see these men, who have come here to rescue the people from this accursed bondage, driven out and do nothing to assist them? No, I will defy the despot and these men shall preach in my house and Brigham Young may help himself."

The Josephites have held their meetings in our house all winter. At first they were very thinly attended but as the missionaries were very enthusiastic and preached boldly the people gained courage and large numbers flocked to hear the "old faith," which they had first embraced. The numbers increased so much that the house would not hold the people and they spread into the street. Then the minions of Brigham began to annoy them. I sent word to Gen. Connor that peaceable citizens were being disturbed when holding services on the Sabbath and requested him to afford them protection. The next Sabbath about a dozen "boys in blue" came down and mixed among the congregation. Gen. Connor then furnished a large government tent which was put up in my yard about four feet from the house.

In this tent the meetings were afterwards held and large numbers joined the re-organized Church of Jesus Christ of Latter Day Saints.

During this time, I was subjected to many petty annoyances. My door-key was stolen and I could not lock the front door. One evening one of Brigham's boys attended church and stole my dried beef. I started with one of the Josephites to follow him but he slid through the fence and disappeared. One of the children was out playing with the children of a mormon family and heard a man say that "they would burn down that d—d old tent to-night." I sat up expecting every minute to see the flames blaze up. It was about 11 o'clock. I was up looking over letters and papers and listening intently. I heard footsteps on the porch. Two men were there and trying to ascertain if anybody was awake. I had a dim light burning but the shutters were closed very tight. I could look out but they could see nothing inside. My heart stood still and I was riveted to my seat. I thought a moment and recollected that the front door was not locked and that if they chose they could step right into the house. I was very well acquainted with a mormon priest who lived across the way and knew that he secretly sympathized with the Josephites and so I sprang to my feet and rushed to the door and with great noise and a show of bravery I did not feel, opened the door and rushed out. The men taken by surprise by the sudden movement sprang over the bannisters and disappeared in the bushes. I ran across to the High Priest's house, called him up and we went in search of the marauders. Nothing could be found of them and so I watched until daybreak before lying down to get a little rest. Next day I sent to Gen. Connor and told him he must either protect the property of the Government or take it away.

He sent down a guard after that who slept in the tent and also protected my house and family.

He twice prepared quarters for me at Camp Douglas thinking it extremely dangerous for me to remain among the mormons, subject as I was to Brigham's bitter hate. I was denounced in the "Deseret News" and threatened in every covert way in order to frighten me into leaving the city for Brigham said he would rather have forty gentile men, than one gentile woman among his people.

Gen. Connor caused to be conveyed to Brigham the information that "If any of the Federal officers or their families were again disturbed or annoyed by his people he should have only twenty minutes to get his women and children out of the Harem, before he would turn his cannon on to the Prophet's premises and raze his buildings to the ground." My friends importuned me to leave the city and go to Camp Douglas. I refused saying, "I am an American Citizen on

American soil and under the protection of the Stars and Stripes, and I will not be driven, and I demand protection for myself and family until I am ready to leave the Territory." The battle of words and pens waxed hot. The "Deseret News" vs. "The Vedette," a paper in the interest of the Federal officers and the military. During the hottest of the fight a grand review was held at Camp Douglas. The Cavalry were out in all their glory and the Infantry marched and counter-marched, pretty close to the city. The guns were drawn close to the city and pointed either by design or otherwise in the direction of the Harem. Great excitement prevailed and again the flag of distress was given to the breeze on the Lion House. The women came running to me in tears begging that I would use my influ- ence to avert the impending calamity. I told them to go home and I would see they were not injured. Meantime the Josephites increased in numbers and "ceased not daily to teach the word baptizing in the river Jordan" all those who would be saved from the fatal heresy of Brigham and his accomplices.

But the tyrant was not idle, for in every way known to savage cruelty he persecuted these poor people. He ordered the Bishops to "kick them out of their wards" to get up quarrels with them cut them off from the church and turn them over to the buffetings of Satan. The formula is,

"In the name, and by the authority of the Holy Priesthood, which I possess, I cut you off from the church and curse you from the crown of your head to the soles of your feet and turn you over to the buffetings of Satan for a thousand years, and pronounce upon you and your children and your children's children, the curse of Almighty God. May your crops wither and your lands become parched with drouth; may your family cry for bread with none to succor; may your substance vanish, and your life become a burden; may you be cursed in your members; and may you find no pleasure in life, and unless you repent may your blood be shed for the remission of your sins, in order that your soul be saved alive. In the name of the Priesthood and with the sanction of Almighty God, Amen."

These "Saints" are so devout that they have many ways of assisting the Almighty in carrying out his threats. One poor man had a nice little farm and garden and was doing well when he embraced the Josephite faith. The Bishop soon had a quarrel pitched with him about his title to the land. He had in the Reformation, as it is here called, consecrated his property to the church or in other words deeded it to Brigham

Young as Trustee in Trust. This gave the Bishop the right to take possession. The owner was obliged to give it up and look up another home.

Another man could get no water for his farm and of course the Lord cursed it with drouth.

This country is watered entirely by irrigation, and the ditches are owned by the church and if a man is not in good standing he can get no water. When a man is beyond hope of repentance and they get him out in secret they disable him in such a way, as to render him miserable for life.

If a man apostatizes who possesses secrets which would be very damaging to the Church they have such a lively interest in his soul that they shed his blood on the altar of sacrifice. Many a man and woman have gone into the Endowment House, and have never come out, and their friends know well their fate, but so terrible is the fear and so closely are they watched that they are dumb.

There are now about three hundred Josephites who desire to leave the territory and the government has ordered Gen. Connor to furnish them an escort of mounted men. Several of them have some money which they have placed in camp for safety and which the mormons have tried to steal. Everything that could be got away from them they have taken and but for the generosity of the government they would be destitute of the means of living.

As there will be nothing more that I can do after these people get away I shall leave Salt Lake about the same time they do. Mr. Burlingame has concluded to remain in Idaho and has resigned his office and requested the Governor to send his family to him and furnish them with an escort, as it would be unsafe to travel through the country without.

Gen. Connor is about sending out a company of Cavalry to hunt Indians, and says if I will go along as far as they go he will furnish me a wagon and make the family as comfortable as possible and furnish me an escort of mounted men from there on. I have accepted his proposition and will be ready to go when the company start. I told the General that I had seen about everything else in this western life except an Indian fight and I thought I would try that now.

Well, at last I have turned my back on the Saints. The Josephites got away yesterday morning and a happier set of people I never saw than they were when everything was ready for a start with the government escort of mounted men to accompany them. If the strong arm of the law could be kept on Brigham and his willing dupes for a few years this whole perplexing question could be settled. Two thirds of the people would embrace original Mormonism and become industrious and law abiding citizens.

This morning bright and early my escort rode up with the establishment which is to convey myself and family to Idaho City. The "boys" soon got everything aboard and bidding my good friends from Camp Douglas farewell I gladly shook the dust of Salt Lake City from my feet and started on my perilous journey. As the sun went down I turned my eyes once more to look upon one of the loveliest sights I ever beheld.

The Great Salt Lake lay like a beautiful mirror reflecting the mountains in their grandeur and verdure upon its clear bosom. The "City of the Saints" with its broad streets, with lofty shade trees on either side, and singing rivulets of water flowing down each side-walk, its well built houses, its lovely gardens full of sweet scented shrubs and blossoming trees, lay snugly nested in the valley below, forming a picture never to be forgotten. But alas that this Eden of beauty should be cursed with the Upas of death! That despotism of the worst form should here be found, that the lives and property of all the citizens are absolutely under the control of one man and that man a monster of iniquity! Alas that here in this lovely valley the most revolting crimes are sanctioned by a religion that holds its votaries like the vice of hell. 'Tis true that to the eye of a stranger everything appears lovely but like the whited sepulcher "within it is full of dead men's bones." A true home is a stranger to this valley, marriage is stripped of every sentiment that makes it holy, innocent and pure.

Man is a monster of selfishness and lust, and woman is his victim. When I have looked into the faces of these women and have seen the hopeless, lifeless, woe-begone expression there, or the indifferent, even reckless look, my heart has yearned to help them in some way to extricate themselves from this cruel bondage. Farewell, my poor sisters, do not despair, "there will yet arise a light out of darkness."

I bid good bye to the lovely valley and its people, to the many kind hearts and true, that it contains and turn to new and untried scenes feeling that there is still danger and adventure in the future as great and exciting as in the past.

THE END.

APPENDIX.

A PANORAMIC VIEW OF MORMONISM.

CHRONOLOGICAL HISTORY.

1805. December 23. Joseph Smith, jun., born at Sharon, Windsor county, Vermont.

1815. April. His father and family remove to Palmyra, Wayne county, New York.

1820. March. Many revivals of religion in western New York, and Smith's mind becomes disturbed.
Under the preaching of Rev. Mr. Lane he becomes partial to the Methodists.

April. Smith pretends to receive his first vision while praying in the woods. He asserts that God the Father and Jesus Christ came to him from the heavens; and, like Mohammed's Gabriel, told him that his sins were forgiven; that he was the chosen of God to reinstate his kingdom and re-introduce the gospel; that none of the denominations were right, etc.

1823. September 21. Smith says that an angel came to him while he was in bed, and told him of the existence and preservation of the history of the ancient inhabitants of America, engraved on plates of gold, and directed him where to find them.

September 22. Goes as directed and discovers them in a stone box, in a hill side between Manchester and Palmyra, western New York. He attempts to take them, but is prevented. The devil and angels contend about him; devil is whipped and retreats: he receives many instructions from the angel and begins preparing himself for his future.

1827. January 18. Smith married to Miss Emma Hale, afterward "Lady elect of the Church."

1829. April 17. Translation recommenced, Oliver Cowdery acting as clerk.

May 5. Smith states that John the Baptist came and ordained Cowdery and himself "priests;" and commanded them "to baptize and afterward re-ordain each other."

1830. Smith was ordained Apostle by Peter, James, and John.

April 6. The Mormon Church organized at Manchester, New York, and consisted of J. Smith, sen., Hiram and Samuel Smith, O. Cowdery, Joseph Knight and J. Smith, jun. Martin Harris, one of the witnesses, not being one among them!

1830. June. First conference at Fayette, New York.

August. Parley P. Pratt and Sidney Rigdon converted to Mormonism.

December. Smith is visited by Rigdon.

1831. January. The Church commanded to move to Kirtland, Ohio, where Rigdon had a body of persons converted to Mormonism as a nucleus.

May. The Elders sent out by twos to preach.

June 7. The first endowment given; Elders much disappointed in their expectations. Many ordained and sent out to preach. New branches growing up rapidly.

June 17. Smith and party start for Missouri to search for a location for "Zion."

August 3. Zion determined to be in Independence, Jackson county, Mo. Smith dedicates the "Temple block;" names the place "The New Jerusalem," and returns to Kirtland.

August 27. "The Kirtland Safety Society Bank," store, mill, and other mercantile operations commenced by Smith.

1832. February 16. Smith and Sidney Rigdon pretend to see in a vision the whole destiny of man, and his different degrees of glory and punishment.

March 22. Smith mobbed, tarred and feathered for dishonorable dealing.

April 2. Smith visits Jackson county, Mo., where matters are in disorder.

1833. March 8. The first presidency organized by the appointment of Sidney Rigdon and Frederic G. Williams as Smith's counselors.

July 23. The foundation of Kirtland Temple laid by Smith. The mob at Independence, Jackson county, Mo., rise against the Mormons, and extort a promise of half to leave by January, and all by April, 1834.

October 30. The mob destroys ten Mormon houses. Two of the mobbers are killed by the Saints. This was the first blood shed, and the Mormons shed it.

November. The Mormons fly from Jackson, and are kindly received in Clay county, Mo.

1834. February 20. Smith goes with companies from Kirtland to Missouri, to the relief of the Saints; organizes a small army, and begins to dream of physical conquest and temporal sovereignty.

May 4. Mormon Church first called "The Church of Jesus Christ of Latter-Day Saints" by Sidney Rigdon at a convention at Kirtland.

July 9. Smith returns to Kirtland, where his presence began to be needed.

1835. February 14. The first quorum of the Twelve Apostles ordained at Kirtland; and among them Brigham Young and Heber C. Kimball.

Classes of instruction and school of Prophets commenced. Sidney Rigdon delivers six lectures on Faith generally attributed to J. Smith, being unaccredited to their author, and bound in the book of Smith's Revelations [Doctrines and Covenants].

1836. March 27. The Kirtland Temple, finished at a cost of $40,000, is dedicated; at which Smith pretends to see Moses, Elias, and Elijah, who give him different "keys" of priesthood, which guarantied to their possessors unlimited power in spiritual and temporal things.

1837. June 1. O. Hyde and Kimball appointed to go to England as missionaries.

November. Smith's Kirtland Safety Society Bank broke, store seized, goods sold, and himself insolvent.

1838. January 12. Smith and Rigdon run away in the night from their creditors in Ohio, who were threatening their arrest for fraud.

July 4. Sidney Rigdon, in an anniversary oration, familiarly called by the Mormons "Sidney's Salt Sermon," threatens the Mormon enemies and apostates with physical violence.

1838. July 4. The Danite Band, or United Brothers of Gideon, organized, and placed under the command of David Patten, an Apostle, who assumed the alias of Captain Fearnot.

September 30. The militia, to avenge the death of their comrades, brutally attack the Mormon women and children at Hawn's Mill, shooting them down and burning the houses, and committing other barbarous atrocities on the women.

November. The Saints are kindly received at Quincy, Illnois.

Smith arrested and about to be shot by the excited military, but is handed over to the civil authorities and is subsequently released.

1839. March 25. Brigham Young and others relay the foundation of the Temple at Independence, Jackson county, Mo.

May 9. Smith goes to Commerce, Ill., by invitation of Dr. Isaac Galland, of whom he obtains gratis a large tract of land, to induce him to settle there with the people.

CHRONOLOGICAL HISTORY. 297

September. Brigham Young, H. C. Kimball and others leave for England as missionaries; O. Hyde although previously appointed by "revelation," not accompanying them.

October. Smith and others go to Washington, to try and obtain redress from Congress for their injuries in Missouri.

The town of Commerce chosen a "Stake of Zion" by Smith.

1840. April 21. Commerce changes its name to Nauvoo.

October 3. Mormons begin preparing to build the Temple, and petition the State Legislature of Illinois for the incorporation of Nauvoo.

1841. February 4. Nauvoo incorporation act, passed in the preceding winter, begins to be in force. Nauvoo Legion organized. J. Smith, Lieutenant-General.

April 6. The foundation stones of Nauvoo Temple laid by Smith, with grand military parade.

1842. May 6. Governor L. W. Boggs of Missouri shot at by Orrin Porter Rockwell [now at Salt Lake City].

1844. February 7. J. Smith, as a candidate for the Presidency of U. S., issues his address.

May 6. Smith and party destroy the material of "The Expositor."

June 24. The arms are demanded from the citizens of Nauvoo by the Governor of Illinois.

June 27. Joseph Smith, Jr., and his brother Hiram are shot in jail at Carthage, Illinois, by a gang of Missourians.

August 15. The Twelve Apostles, with Brigham Young at their head, assume the presidency of the Church; and address, as such, an epistle to the "Saints in all the world."

October 7. Brigham Young's authority is fully recognized by the majority of the Mormon people. Rigdon and all the contumacious members cut off, cursed, "and delivered to the devil to be buffeted in the flesh for a thousand years!" by Brigham.

1845. January. Nauvoo charter is repealed by the State Legislature.

February. Brigham Young and the Mormon authorities begin to seriously contemplate a general move to the west.

. John Taylor, an Apostle, proposes Van Couver's Island, in British America. Lyman Wright, also then an Apostle, proposes Texas. Others suggest California, then but little known. Much dissension as to locality. Some valley in the Rocky Mountains finally selected.

May. The cap-stone of the Mormon Temple laid: endowments soon after begin.

1846. January. Baptism for the dead administered in the River Mississippi.

20. Pioneers leave Nauvoo to find some resting-place on the borders of Iowa. They select Council Bluffs.

February. Mormon companies cross the ice-covered river *en route* for Council Bluffs.

July. Brigham Young sells a company of his brethren as a Mexican Battalion, for $20000.

September. Nauvoo, in which many of the Mormons were remaining, besieged by the mob.

1847. April 14. The pioneers leave their winter quarters, Council Bluffs, Iowa, for the Rocky Mountains, and by following the trail of Col. Fremont, arrive at Salt Lake.

July 23. Orson Pratt and a few arrive at the valley.

24. Brigham and main body of pioneers enter. This day, instead of the 23d, is always celebrated, as a compliment to Brigham, a species of sycophancy very customary from the Mormon people toward the Mormon Prophet.

December 24. Brigham Young nominated "President of the Church of Jesus Christ of Latter Day Saints in all the World," at a special conference. He appoints Heber C. Kimball and Willard Richards as his coadjutors.

1848. April. 6. His appointment confirmed at the General Conference at Kanesville, Iowa.

May. The Saints start for Salt Lake City, where they arrive in the fall.

CHRONOLOGICAL HISTORY. 299

1849. March 5. Convention held at Salt Lake City; Constitution of State of Deseret drafted by them, and Legislature elected under its provisions.

July 2. They send delegates to Washington to present Constitution and Petition for admission into the Union as a "sovereign and independent State."

August. Capt. Stansbury, T. E., arrived, to make survey of the valleys, and of Salt Lake.

September 9. Bill organizing Utah Territory, signed by President Fillmore.

1850. February. Brigham takes oath of office as Governor of Utah Territory and Superintendent of Indian Affairs, having been appointed by President Fillmore.

April 5. Assembly met, and State of Deseret was merged into Territory of Utah.

June 5. "Deseret News" commenced, under editorial charge of Dr. Willard Richards, "a prophet, seer, and revelator."

September. Judges Brochus, Day, Brandenburg, and Mr. Secretary Harris arrive at Salt Lake.

22. Mr. Brochus insults the people. Brigham threatens violence, and the Judges leave Utah.

1851. The Salt Lake Tabernacle built.
1853. February 14. Temple excavations commenced.
April 6. Corner stones of Temple laid.
1854. August. Colonel Steptoe and soldiers arrive at Utah.
1855. May. Colonel Steptoe, having resigned the governorship of Utah, left with troops for California.

August. Judge Drummond, General Burr, Surveyor-General, and other U. S. officials arrive at Salt Lake.

1856. May. Judge Drummond left.
1857. The mormons in open rebellion.

July. Governor A. Cumming, Chief Justice D. R. Eckels, Associate Justices, John Cradlebaugh and Charles E. Sinclair, and Sec. John Hartnett, appointed.

September. An army of 3000 men is armed and

equipped, and ordered to march for Utah under command of Col. A. S. Johnston. The Mountain Meadow massacre. Brigham Young declares martial law.

1858. The Mormons victorious and the Governor and President outwitted. The Mormons graciously accept pardon and deign to allow the troops to pass through Salt Lake City in safety.

The Mormon war, costing twenty millions a disgraceful fiasco. Cumming nominated Governor. The "war" over, the Courts undertake to do business but are frustrated and prevented as usual by the mormons. Judge Cradlebaugh attempts to bring the perpetrators of the Mountain Meadow massacre to punishment but fails.

1860. John F. Kinney appointed Chief Justice to succeed Eckels. Judges Crosby and Flenniken, appointed. October. John W. Dawson appointed to succeed Cumming as Governor. The mormons get a "hook in his nose" and send him flying out of the Territory.

1862. Stephen S. Harding appointed Governor. Thomas J. Drake and Charles B. Waite appointed Associate Justices. The Anti-Polygamy Bill passed. The Governor's message denouncing Polygamy. Mormons indignant. Judge Waite draws a Bill to amend the Organic act which causes great excitement among the mormons. An indignation meeting held and the Governor and Judges denounced and threatened and asked to resign.

These officers decline to leave. Mob violence.

1863. Hon. John Titus appointed to succeed Chief Justice Kinney, elected as Delegate to Congress from Utah.

Jan. 29. Gen. Connor fights the battle of Bear River. Brigham Young takes another wife.

1864. James Duane Doty appointed to succeed Harding. Governor Doty's death.

1865. Charles Durkee his Successor.

1869. Col. Shafer appointed Governor.

CHRONOLOGICAL HISTORY.

1872. George L. Woods appointed to succeed Shafer.
1875. July 1. George W. Emery appointed.
1880. Jan. 27. Eli H. Murray, Governor.
1882. March 15. The Edmunds Anti-polygamy Bill passed both houses of Congress. Signed by President Arthur.

SUBSTANCE OF THE BILL.

The main provisions of the Edmund Bill are: That any person who has a wife living, who marries again in a Territory, is subject to a fine of not more than $500 and to imprisonment not more than five years; that any male person in a Territory who cohabits with more than one woman, is subject to a fine of not more than $300, or to imprisonment for not more than six months, or to both fine and imprisonment; that any person who has been living in the practice of bigamy, polygamy or unlawful cohabitation with more than one woman, may be challenged as a juror, in trials under this and similar laws; or he may be challenged if he believes these acts to be right; that the President may grant amnesty to those who have committed any of these offences before the passage of this act; that the issue of Mormon marriages born before January 1st 1883, are legitimate; that no person guilty of either of these offences shall be entitled to vote or hold office in any Territory; that a board of five persons is to be appointed, who are to make all necessary provisions for an election of a new Legislative Assembly, to be composed of persons qualified according to this act.

WHAT THE MORMOMS THINK OF IT.

Salt Lake, March 15.—The DESERET NEWS says of the Edmunds bill: "It is regarded by the Mormon people as a scheme to place the control of public offices in Utah in the hands of the Gentiles—not as an honest attempt to suppress polygamy. The only concern felt is with regard to the provisions which will affect all classes alike, rather than those which are ostensibly aimed at polygamy, for the former are a departure from the Constitution, and the purpose manifested to disregard its limitations in order to break down a religious organization argues an entire departure, at no distant day, from the principles upon which the safety of this Government depends. The thing over which the country has enraged itself will remain comparatively untouched. The people who have been holding meetings and signing petitions had one thing in view, the framers of the Edmunds bill another. It will be found that the public has been fooled, while the plotting politicians have succeeded so far in their endeavors. But, though they have apparently gained a victory, time and the workings of the law will evolve troubles that they have not counted upon, and there is a power at work in Mormonism which they always leave out of their calculations. That power is beyond the control of Congress and courts, and will, in the future as in the past, overrule every thing that is done or attempted, so that it will redound to the benefit of the system and the good of its adherents."

We are again, after more than thirty years of temporizing and trifling, face to face with the Mormon problem. When Millard Fillmore in 1850, signed the bill erecting Utah into a Territory and endorsed the infamy by making Brigham Young its Governor, he gave countenance and character to the worst form of domestic tyranny, and struck a blow at republican institutions which he regretted to his dying day.

From that day to the present time the Government has been hood-winked and out-witted by these people and it remains to be seen whether Congress has not again left a loop-hole through which these oily, wily and desperate leaders will manage to slip and evade the law and still carry on their nefarious system in spite of all law.

The Territorial Legislature has always been in Utah, like the fifth wheel to a coach; the Legislature of the "State of Deseret," being the de facto law making power. The "State Legislature," being composed of the same parties, meets and passes all laws and upon its adjournment the Territorial Legislature convenes and sanctions what the former have done, not because they consider it of any more binding force but in order to keep up appearances, and draw the Government money. Hereafter, if these old polygamists cannot control the Territoral Legislature they will entirely ignore it. But they will control it because they have the money and influence to do it.

A large majority of the Mormon men have never been in Polygamy and never desire to be.

The leaders do not encourage it. Only the faithful few who can be trusted and made useful are allowed more than one wife. The most desirable women are appropriated by a few prominent men and hence so many single men in Utah. . They will not take the leavings. Undoubtedly all the marriageable women have been rushed through the endowment and sealed to some of these prominent men. As the present bill is not retroactive they will be all right and will be in a position to seek some way of foiling the government before there is another relay of wives ready. Desperate diseases require desperate remedies and it is greatly to be feared that some treatment more radical and severe will be necessary, to remove from our body politic this loathsome cancer which is making fearful inroads on our political life.

Polygamy involves many difficulties not apparent. The Nihilism of Russia is the nearest to a parallel with Utah Mormonism in America.

What we see and know is not what we have to fear. A most thoroughly organized secret police, penetrating into every nook and corner and showing its hideous work where we had least looked for it, is the real power with which we have to deal. When traveling in an Indian country there is nothing to fear so long as the savages come around your tent and beg or steal whatever they can find, but when you are in their country and you see nothing of them it is then that picket guards are thrown out and every precaution taken.

The first great barrier against the overthrow of

Polygamy is the power of wealth; when a move was made in 1863, to arrest Young for violating the law of 1862, the Gentile merchants, and officers of the overland mail and telegraph companies were very active and zealous in their efforts to quiet the affair, and they succeeded.

The Indians are all in league with the Mormons. They are the lost Ten Tribes, according to the Book of Mormon, and they have nearly all embraced the faith, and taken their endowments and are ready to obey the commands of the leaders at a moments notice. Nearly all the murders laid to Indians, have been ordered and engineered by the Mormon SECRET ORDERS, the Indians merely acting as stool pigeons for them. This was notably the case with the Mountain Meadow massacre.

The latest example of this principle was at or near Fort Apache in September last, in which many valuable lives were lost. From the report in the San Francisco Chronicle we quote:

Tucson, Sept. 3. Fort Apache, near where the massacre occurred, is 210 miles from Tucson. The country is mountainous and full of canons, suitable for ambushing and surprising the enemy. There are many strongholds in the mountains, in which a mere handful of determined men could successfully resist the advance of a hundred times their number. The Apache country is settled almost entirely by mormons, and it is reported here that there is an understanding between them and the Indians. The excitement in Tucson is intense, and there is talk of organizing a force of volunteers and proceeding against the San Carlos Agency. Universal indignation is expressed at the conduct of Indian-Agent Tiffany. He has studiously denied that there was any danger of trouble, and repeatedly asserted that none of the agency Indians were off the reservation.

It is claimed by those well informed in the matter that so large a body of Indians could not be absent without knowledge of the agent, and had he informed the military of the fact, the disaster would doubtless have been averted.

From the above, it is evident that the agent was either a mormon or altogether in the interest of the mormons. Gen. Carr participated in the expedition against the Mormons in 1858 and in 1859 in the expedition against the Kiowas and Comanches and was at Fort Wichita, when the war of the Rebellion broke out. Since the close of the war he has done most excellent service against the Indians, in different parts of the west. Mormons and Indians both held a grudge against him and as neither ever forget an injury they seized the first good opportunity to get even with him.

PRESIDENT GARFIELD AND THE MORMONS.
GUITEAU A MORMON.

It is well known that President Garfield was unalterably opposed to Utah mormonism and that he was doubly pledged to put his foot on it.

We cannot positively affirm that he lost his

life because he was thus opposed, but we will give some reasons why this might be so. The following is from the Chicago Morning News, Oct. 1st 1881.

"The mormons of Colorado, Texas and New Mexico, are greatly elated over the success of Guiteau or Utah as they call him. A mormon preacher, Dr. Sauntry, who passed down the Colorado on a lecturing tour says "that Guiteau acted under orders from head quarters when he shot the President." He also said that more deaths would follow if Guiteau was hanged.

"In 1871, Guiteau joined the Mormons, in Southern Utah where he had plural wives. When the Mormons saw that Garfield in his inaugural said that he would put his foot on polygamy, the leaders at Salt Lake were heard to say, 'Yes, if we do not put our foot on him first.'

"The names of twenty traveling brethren, as such men as Guiteau are called, were selected. The lot fell on Guiteau.

It was against the wishes of the leaders to shoot, they preferring poison or train wrecking. Guiteau said, 'I know my business,' and was allowed to concoct his own devilish plan. The Mormons are determined to fight in defense of what they term their rights, and are willing, if cornered, to die martyrs to their holy cause. Serious apprehension is felt all through the Southwest, where the Mormons' greatest strength is, and the American citizens who live among them are afraid to speak a word against their villainous theories. The mormon dress is not different from that of any other citizen through the States and it is a difficult matter to tell when we are met by one of that lawless mob who intend, as they say, even at the expense of thousands of lives, to fight their way into recognition by the nations of the world as a people who have rights which others must respect."

The fact that Guiteau has constantly persisted that he was doing the will of God and that he was inspired to commit the murder is exactly in keeping with the spirit and teachings of Mormonism. He is very religious, studies the Bible, prays and continually claims to have been acting under the direction of the Almighty in "removing President Garfield." If Guiteau is not insane and is a mormon, his conduct would be fully explained. President Garfield was a bitter foe, and had been ever since the "Saints" were driven from Ohio. He was known to be a man who would carry out his pledges and who would not be driven from his purposes by threats or gold. Hence he was a dangerous man for the Saints to deal with. The opposition of the Stalwarts! the revenge of Guiteau needed only to be inflamed by the idea that the people of God were to be preserved by the death of this powerful ruler and that a "thus saith the Lord," was to justify him, to make a motive powerful enough for the commission of any crime.

Brigham Young Still Alive.

In the Chicago Tribune of March 3d, we find the following:

"Omaha, Neb., March 3. A man from Salt Lake visiting in this city, in the course of animated conversation on the anti-mormon movement, said he believed that Brigham Young is still alive. He said he saw the body which was supposed to be that of the Mormon leader, and, while it might have borne some slight resemblance to that of Brigham Young, it was in reality that of some other person. He knew of a hundred Latter-Day Saints who also failed to recognize the body as that of Young. He had heard Brigham Young often predict that he should be resurrected from the dead, and he firmly believes that when the crisis arrives in the affairs of the Mormons, the resurrection dodge will be played upon the ignorant, superstitious, and fanatical people who compose the Mormon Church. This cunning plan will be in keeping with the various tricks and pretensions that have characterized the Mormon Church since its inception. Brigham Young, a shrewd and far-seeing man, knew that the day was not far off when a vigorous crusade would be made on the Mormon Church, and he adopted the resurrection game, to be put into operation at a time when the people shall need something in the shape of a miracle to firmly cement them together to fight to maintain the principles of the faith.

The man who made these statements is a mormon, but not polygamist. He is what is known as a Josephite, or a believer in the true Mormon Church founded by Joseph Smith, and he denies with all Josephites, that polygamy was ever a part of the Mormon faith preached by Smith.

He is extensively engaged in business in Utah, and is regarded as a man of sound judgment and veracity. While here he visited some of the Josephites, and it was to them that he made revelations of the plan by which Brigham Young is to create the greatest sensation of modern times. He had many business dealings with him. He asserts, with the complete organization and secret workings of the Church, it would be an easy matter to keep Brigham Young concealed for almost any length of time, and reproduce him when most needed to revive the faith of believers by his apparent resurrection. That his resurrection would be taken as a matter of fact there is no doubt, and the superstitious people would follow the Prophet's banner with the zeal of fanatics and shed their blood in its defense. This Josephite's statement is to some extent confirmed by a retired army officer, who was on most friendly and intimate terms with Brigham Young. This officer, who viewed the alleged remains of Young, has, it is said, made the assertion that it did not bear the slightest resemblance to Brigham Young."

Brigham Young's death occurred just at the time when a warrant was out for his arrest for complicity in the Mountain Meadow massacre. He was only sick about twenty-four hours. An attack of cholera morbus is said to have been his disease, but he was one of the most careful and abstemious of men.

When Judge Cradlebaugh undertook to bring to justice those concerned in the Mountain Meadow and other massacres, a great many of the mormon leaders fled to Mount Kolob, or the residence of the Gods. This is in a very mountainous region, and almost inaccessible.

Here they remained until the storm blew over and it was safe to return. For many years the mormons have been accummulating wheat and other provisions in certain caves and hiding places to be ready in case of a siege, and I have heard them say that they could live in the mountains for twenty years. If Brigham Young is still alive, and those who are the best acquainted with mormon tactics will be the most ready to believe it, he is most likely in one of the Islands of the Pacific. It has long been well understood among the leading polygamists that when the United States government could no longer be trifled with, and they had to go, that they would settle in one of those balmy Isles of the calm Pacific and establish a kingdom all their own, where they could pass the evening of their days in calm serenity, untroubled by the 'cursed gentiles.' To this end they have had extensive missions in those Islands and have converted many of the inhabitants to their religion, which would not be difficult to do since they are already polygamists. It requires therefore no great stretch of the imagination, to see Brigham Young sitting on his throne of state in splendor, surrounded by his slaves and satellites, and having a harem rivaling in extent that of the Sultan himself.

Whenever, therefore, these shrewd and wily old polygamists make up their minds that the people of the United States are really in earnest and that the power and machinery of the government will be turned against them, and their wives and children and property confiscated, and they deprived of their liberties, then and not until then they will go.

OUR BOOKS.

NOW READY.

ADVENTURES
IN THE
FAR WEST;
AND
LIFE AMONG THE MORMONS.
BY
MRS. C. V. WAITE,

Author of "THE MORMON PROPHET and HIS HAREM," "THE LAW of SOCIAL RETRIBUTION," "WOMAN'S POSITION in CHURCH and STATE," etc. etc.

If you want to be entertained by reading hair-breadth escapes, attacks by Indians, crossing rivers, perilous ascents and descents of mountains;

READ this BOOK.

If you want to learn all about the true inwardness of MORMONISM read "ADVENTURES in the FAR WEST."

If you want to know how the MORMON POLYGAMIST lives among his many wives, read this BOOK.

It gives a full account of "THE HAREM, PROPHET'S BLOCK, BRIGHAM'S WIVES; how the Women look; how they live; how they endure the horrors of Polygamy."

If you want to read a good story, send for the ADVENTURES.

350 pp. handsomely bound in cloth.

Only, $1.00. The usual discount to the trade. Send orders to C. V. WAITE, & COMPANY.

33 MAJOR BLOCK, 143, LASALLE ST.

CHICAGO.

AND BOOK SELLERS GENERALLY.

1882.

Price, post-paid, $1.00.

Special rates for fifty copies and upwards, in one order, to one address.

HISTORY OF THE CHRISTIAN RELIGION, to the year 200. Price, $2.25.

MARIAN LEE, or One Woman's Trials and Triumphs: By Mrs. M. E. DE GEER. Price, $1.00.

THE HISTORY of the TEMPERANCE REFORM, by REV. JAMES SHAW. 530 pp. Price, $2.00.

THE DEFENCE of FREE MASONRY, by MRS. M. E. DE GEER. Price, bound in cloth, $1.00.

Any of the above sent, post-paid, on receipt of price. To accommodate our patrons we will send any book to be had in Chicago, promptly.

Send us an order.

C. V. WAITE & COMPANY.

Illinois Central R. R.

THE SHORTEST, QUICKEST, AND ONLY DIRECT
Route between
CHICAGO AND NEW ORLEANS,
MEMPHIS, VICKSBURG AND MOBILE.

The only Route running
PALACE SLEEPING CARS
THROUGH BETWEEN
Chicago and N. Orleans, without change.

THE QUICKEST ROUTE BETWEEN
CHICAGO and ST. LOUIS
WITHOUT CHANGE OF CARS.

PALACE SLEEPING CARS between CHICAGO and ST. LOUIS, making direct connections at St. Louis, in Union Depot to and from Kansas City, Atchison, Leavenworth, St. Joseph, and all points West.

The Shortest and only ROUTE between CHICAGO and CAIRO *without CHANGE of CARS.*

Making direct connections at CAIRO (or St. Louis,) to and from LITTLE ROCK, HOT SPRINGS, DALLAS, FORT WORTH, HOUSTON, GALVESTON & SAN ANTONIA.

THIS IS THE SHORTEST ROUTE between
CHICAGO AND ARKANSAS AND TEXAS.

A Direct Route to Springfield, Peoria and Keokuk, without change of CARS.

For Tickets and information, apply at the I. C. R. R. Ticket Office, 121 Randolph Street (near Clark), and at the Depot, foot of Lake Street.

A. H. HANSON,
Gen'l Passenger Agent.

TAKE THE
CHICAGO
BURLINGTON & QUINCY
RAIL ROAD,

Burlington Route.

IT IS THE GREAT

THROUGH CAR LINE

From CHICAGO to all Points in the

WEST AND SOUTH WEST,

AND IS THE

FINEST EQUIPPED

RAIL ROAD
IN THE

WORLD.

T. J. POTTER, } PERCEVAL LOWELL,
Gen'l Manager. } Gen'l Passenger Ag't.

CHICAGO.

THREE GREAT CITIES of the WEST.

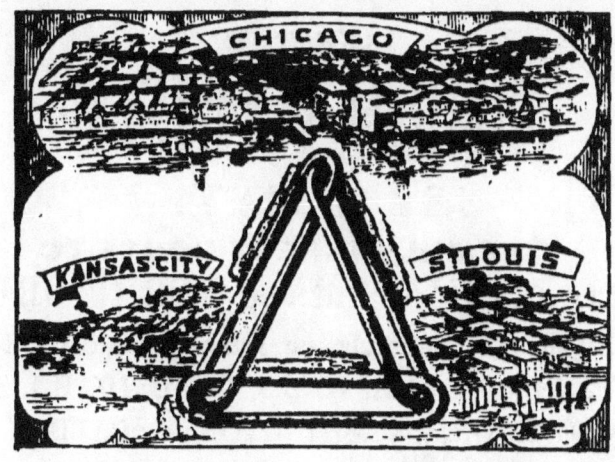

LINKED TOGETHER BY THE
Chicago & Alton R. R.

No Change of Cars OF ANY CLASS BETWEEN } CHICAGO & KANSAS CITY, CHICAGO & ST. LOUIS, AND ST. LOUIS & KANSAS CITY.

Union Depots in EAST ST. LOUIS, ST. LOUIS, KANSAS CITY, and CHICAGO   No other line runs

PALACE DINING CARS

between CHICAGO and KANSAS CITY, CHICAGO and ST. LOUIS, and ST. LOUIS and KANSAS CITY. Meals equal to those served in any First-Class Hotel, only 75 cents.

The finest PALACE RECLINING CHAIR CARS in the world are run in all Through Trains, day and night, without change, and Free of EXTRA CHARGE.

PULLMAN PALACE SLEEPING CARS

the finest, best and safest in use anywhere. The best and quickest route from CHICAGO TO MEMPHIS, MOBILE, NEW ORLEANS, and all points SOUTH via ST. LOUIS.

The Short Line to MISSOURI, ARKANSAS, TEXAS, KANSAS, COLORADO, NEW MEXICO, ARIZONA, NEBRASKA, OREGON, CALIFORNIA, etc. The GREAT EXCURSION ROUTE between the NORTH and SOUTH, and to and from KANSAS LANDS and COLORADO HEALTH RESORTS and MINING DISTRICTS. SEE that your tickets read via "CHICAGO & ALTON RAILROAD." For Maps, Time Tables, &c,, address

JAMES CHARLTON, General Passenger and Ticket Agent, 210 Dearborn St., Corner Adams, CHICAGO.

J. C. McMULLIN, General Manager.

ARE YOU GOING WEST?
TAKE THE
UNION PACIFIC
RAILWAY.
THE ONLY DIRECT ROUTE TO
CALIFORNIA and the TERRITORIES.

All persons contemplating removal to COLORADO, WYOMING, the BLACK HILLS, UTAH, IDAHO, MONTANA, OREGON, WASHINGTON or CALIFORNIA, should correspond with

J. W. MORSE, General Passenger Agt., UNION PACIFIC RAILROAD, Omaha, Nebraska, before purchasing tickets via any other line.

Information of value relative to routes, rates, inducements to settlers, etc., together with carefully prepared and reliable publications descriptive of the STATES and TERRITORIES named, will be mailed FREE, upon application to

J. W. MORSE, General Passenger Agent,
OMAHA, NEBRASKA, or.
D. E. CORNELL,
KANSAS CITY, MISSOURI.

Chicago & Eastern Illinois
RAIL ROAD
AND
DANVILLE ROUTE
TO THE SOUTH AND SOUTHEAST.

Chicago and Nashville Short Line.

Fifty miles the shortest route from Chicago to Nashville, Tennessee, with only ONE CHANGE of cars for ALL CLASSES of passengers, an advantage offered by NO OTHER LINE.

Quick Time and Sure Connections.

ELEGANT SLEEPING CARS

on all night trains—close connections made at Nashville for

CHATTANOOGA,   SAVANNAH.
ATLANTA,   CHARLESTON,
MACON.   JACKSONVILLE,
AUGUSTA,   FERNANDINA

and all other points in

GEORGIA,
SOUTH CAROLINA,
AND FLORIDA.

Parties who intend to visit Florida, should send to the undersigned for "Florida Guide" containing full information in regard to popular resorts., etc, etc., also maps, time tables and full information furnished on application to

A. S. DUNHAM,
Gen'l Passenger and Ticket Agent,
O. S. LYFORD, Superintendent,   CHICAGO.
WM. HILL, Northwestern Passenger Agent.

Chicago & North Western
RAILWAY,

Comprising Trunk Lines to and from

THE WEST AND NORTH WEST.

THE AMERICAN OVERLAND ROUTE,
CHICAGO, COUNCIL BLUFFS
AND CALIFORNIA LINE.

Council Bluffs and Omaha Line; Sioux City and Southern Dakota Line.

TWO ROUTES TO DENVER.

Chicago SAINT PAUL and MINNEAPOLIS Line, via BELOIT and MADISON.

Minnesota and Central Dakota Line, and Huron, Pierre and DEADWOOD Lines.

Milwaukee, Green Bay and Marquette Line; Janesville, Watertown and Fond Du Lac Line.

This is the ONLY Line running PULLMAN PALACE SLEEPING CARS between CHICAGO ST. PAUL & MINNEAPOLIS.

The DINING CAR ROUTE between CHICAGO and COUNCIL BLUFFS and CHICAGO & ST. PAUL.

Ticket Offices in CHICAGO:
62 Clark St. Grand Pacific Hotel. Palmer House and Depot. All Trains from Passenger Station, cor. Wells and Kinzie Sts.

W. H. STENNETT, General Passenger Agent.

www.ingramcontent.com/pod-product-compliance
Lightning Source LLC
Chambersburg PA
CBHW021201230426
43667CB00006B/501